What Do You

Guidance and Exercises in Oral Communication

Andrew Armitage

Senior lecturer in General Studies
Orpington College of Further Education

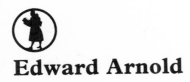

Edward Arnold

©Andrew Armitage 1983

First published 1983
by Edward Arnold (Publishers) Ltd
41 Bedford Square London WC1B 3DQ

Edward Arnold (Australia) Pty Ltd
80 Waverley Road
Caulfield East 3145
PO Box 234
Melbourne

British Library Cataloguing in Publication Data

Armitage, Andrew, *1950–*
  What Do You Say?
  1. Oral communication
  I. Title
  808.5   P9.5

ISBN 0-7131-0721-9

Text set in 11/12pt Plantin Compugraphic
by Colset Private Limited, Singapore.
Printed and bound in Great Britain by Spottiswoode Ballantyne Limited, Colchester and London.

Contents

Teacher's introduction

If insufficient attention has been paid to the teaching of oral communications to students making the transition to the adult world, as many complain it has, this could be because of two difficulties facing teachers: firstly, the feeling that it is arrogant and foolhardy to attempt to teach students about something at which they are experts with at least ten years' experience; secondly, the very real practical problem of how you go about the business of teaching students who, in a classroom, often lack confidence. In relation to the first difficulty, I have found that students, although sophisticated speakers in informal situations which are familiar to them, lack experience of the formal situations they are increasingly finding themselves in as young adults and, as a consequence, have much to learn. In relation to the second, there are ways, using role-play and simulation, of reducing students' embarrassment and therefore reluctance to speak. Further, there is a great deal of work which can be done on non-verbal communication, preparation for speaking, developing an awareness of what leads to misunderstandings, and so on, which does not involve spoken perfomance.

What Do You Say? therefore begins with two units which consider the non-verbal and technical aspects of speech respectively and, in Unit 3, concentrates on the more logical aspects of conveying information and the expression and defence of opinions. Unit 4 looks at the performance situations the students should already be familiar with before Units 5, 6 and 7 take them on to more formal and less familiar situations. In addition, there is a balance throughout the book of performance and non-performance exercises and of single, pair and group work involving role-play and simulation.

The final three sections are assignments based on authentic work situations which involve both spoken and written tasks and attempt to consolidate the work of Units 1–7.

Andrew Armitage

Acknowledgements

I would like to express my thanks to the following who helped in the development of this book: my students, especially those on the BEC and Vocational Preparation courses, and my colleagues Ian Cardall, Margaret Metcalfe and Ruth Shade at Orpington College of Further Education; Plantravel Ltd Sidcup – particularly Diane and Cathy; South East Insurance Brokers Ltd Sidcup; Marks and Spencer Ltd Bromley – in particular Julia Warner and Debbie Brockwell.

The Publishers would like to thank the following organizations for permission to reproduce copyright materials:

Black and Decker Ltd, Cannon Lane, Maidenhead, Berkshire SL6 3PD; National Insurance and Guarantee Corporation Ltd, Citadel House, 5–11 Fetter Lane, London EC4P 4NA; South East Insurance Brokers Ltd, 35 Sidcup Hill, Sidcup, Kent; Wallace-Arnold Tours Ltd, 8 Park Lane, Croydon, CK9 1DN.

The Publishers would also like to thank the following for permission to reproduce the photographs on pages 3–7:
Tish Murta: pages 3, 5, 6, 7;
Barnaby's Picture Library: page 4.

Checklist of objectives

If completed as part of the BEC General People and Communication Module, the assignments in Assignments 1, 2 and 3 are designed to cover General and Learning Objectives as follows:

Assignments 1 South Thames Insurance Brokers

1 A *A New Quote*
General Objectives — A B C D E F H
Learning Objectives — A1, 3 B1 C1 D1, 2 E1, 3 F1, 2 H1

1 B *The Accident Report Form*
General Objectives — A B D E F H
Learning Objectives — A3, B1 D1, 2 E1, 2, 3 F1, 2, 3 H1, 2

1 C *A Claim*
General Objectives — A B E F H
Learning Objectives — A1, 3 B1 E1 F1 H1, 2

Assignments 2 Travel Well Ltd

2 A *Hoverover Ltd*
General Objectives — A B D E F H
Learning Objectives — A1 B1 D1, 2 E1, 3 F1, 2 H1, 2

2 B *Jewels of The North*
General Objectives — A B D E F H
Learning Objectives — A1 B1 D1, 2 E1, 3 F1, 2 H1, 2

2 C *Balance Due*
General Objectives — A B C D E F H
Learning Objectives — A3 B1 C1 D1, 2 E1, 3 F1, 2, 3 H1, 2

2 D *A Complaint*
General Objectives — A B C D E F H
Learning Objectives — A3 B1 C2 D1, 2 E1, 3 F1, 2, 3 H1, 2

Assignments 3 Bendalls Ltd

3 A *Starting at Bendalls*
General Objectives — A B E F H
Learning Objectives — A2 D1, 2 E1, 2 F1, 2, 3 H1, 2

3 B *Stationery*
General Objectives — A B D E F H
Learning Objectives — A3 B1 D1, 2 E1, 2, 3 F1, 2, 3 H1, 2

3 C *A Complaint*
General Objectives — A B C D E F H
Learning Objectives — A3 B1, 2 C1, 2, 3 D1, 2 E1, 2, 3 F1, 2, 3 H1, 2

Unit 1

Self presentation and non-verbal communication

1.1 Self presentation

1 In table 1 are a number of qualities.

On your own Fill in the table below, putting a tick under the number on the scale which most accurately reflects what you think about yourself, eg if you think you're extremely friendly, put a tick under 1 and an extremely unhappy person, tick 5, and so on.

Fill in the table again – only this time, indicate what you think *others* think of you.

	1	2	3	4	5	
Friendly						Unfriendly
Happy						Unhappy
Outgoing						Shy
Eventempered						Quicktempered
Honest						Dishonest
Kind						Unkind
Tolerant						Intolerant
Good sense of humour						No sense of humour
Intelligent						Unintelligent
Likable						Not likable

Since the way we think about ourselves, or our *self image*, is influenced greatly by the way we think *others* see us, it will not be surprising if what you think of yourself and what you consider others think of you, were frequently the same. However, there may be some differences between the ways you filled in the table the first and second times. The differences could imply that you think have a quality but you think others don't see it; or, that you *overestimate* yourself eg you think you're kinder than you actually are; or, that you *underestimate* yourself eg people consider you to be more intelligent than you consider yourself. The differences could also mean, of course, that you're *misreading* people's reactions towards you eg you think you're quite likable but you don't think other people do, when in fact they do like you but you don't realize.

In groups Discuss the differences between people's first and second assessments and try to work out, in each case, why they arise.

On your own Fill in the table a third time, indicating the way you would ideally like to be. Then compare your results with those produced the first time you filled in the table.

You may find that there is no difference in some cases and you're clearly happy about these features of yourself. But in other cases there may be a gap between how you see yourself and what you would prefer to be like.

In groups Discuss the gaps which occurred and whether people feel they could achieve their ideal or not.

On your own One way we arrive at out *self image* is by *comparing* ourselves to others with respect to certain qualities. Write down the name of a person you know or know of, for whom you would give a 1 or 5 rating for each of the qualities in the table above.

2 Our *self image* is influenced, then, by the way others see us but particularly by the ways we're seen in the different groups of people we spend our time with eg our immediate family, school/college/work friends – and so on.

On your own List 5 groups in which you spend your time and, for each, describe briefly how they see you eg as a joker, the life and soul of the party, very quiet, and so on.

In groups Did people find they were seen differently by different groups or as the same person by each group? Did they see themselves in the same way that the groups saw them?

3 First impressions
When we meet someone for the first time, we use clues to build up a picture of what they're like.

2

On your own For each of the following, try to work out:

(i)   What sort of music you think they like.
(ii) How they spend their time.
(iii) How they might talk.
(iv) What interests they have.
(v)   What they're good and bad at.

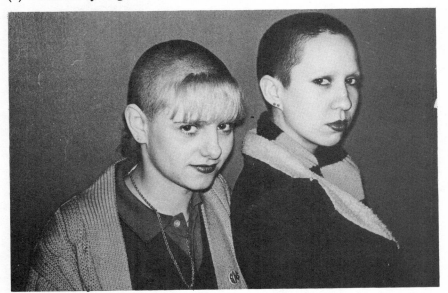

a)

b)

c)

d)

e)

f)

In groups Compare what you wrote down. Was there disagreement or agreement on the whole?
Did a particular photograph produce disagreement?
If so, why?

In groups Judging what people are like on the basis of appearance can lead to *stereotyping* or putting people into a certain class or group. Discuss the possible unfortunate consequences of this.

In pairs Choose 3 of the people from the photographs on pages 3–7. For each, work out a situation in which s/he is misjudged on the basis of first impressions. Then *simulate* each situation.

On your own Knowing people use these clues when they first meet others, write down,

a) how you would present yourself (clothes, hair etc)
    and
b) a description of yourself from the point of view of the person meeting you, in each of the following situations:

(i)   a job interview as an office junior,
(ii) your first day at work in a department store,
(iii) a first visit to a new doctor,
(iv) a local disco/dance,
(v)   a friend's wedding.

Depending on how well we know someone, we often *emphasize* or *conceal* certain aspects of ourselves, eg if you're opening a bank account, you might tend to emphasize that you're a sensible person who spends wisely, is in full control of their finances and who never indulges in reckless spending sprees.

On your own   What aspects would you tend to emphasize and/or conceal in the following situations?

(i)   You're pulled up on your motorcycle by a police officer for a traffic offence.
(ii)   An interview as a cashier.
(iii)   A first night out with a new girl friend/boy friend.
(iv)   An accident occurs and you're the oldest person there.
(v)   Your parents are undecided about whether to let you stay somewhere overnight.

In groups   Did some people tend to emphasize or conceal more than others? Do you consider such behaviour wrong/dishonest?

1.2   Body language

When we talk to people the *body language* we use, or our *non-verbal communication*, is as important as our talk. We use NVC while we talk and while someone else is talking – a situation in which useful information or *feed back* is disclosed to the speaker about what s/he's saying as we listen.

1   Closeness

How close you stand or sit to someone depends on the relationship between you: as a rule the closer the relationship, the closer you tend to stand or sit. However, this is not always true.

On your own   Write down 3 situations in which you wouldn't be alarmed if a complete stranger stood or sat very close to you (eg standing in a lift) and 3 situations in which you would be alarmed.

In groups   Discuss what is common to the first 3 situations and what is common to the second 3 situations.

In groups   The position we choose to sit in when talking to others is important. Two people should take a chair each and, in front of the group, place them near a table and sit down as if the situation were:

(i)   a job interview,
(ii)   an interview at the DHSS,
(iii)   two employees discussing a work problem,

(iv) two friends discussing something they wanted no-one to hear,

(v) two people waiting to be called for a job interview.

Discuss what the differences in positioning were and try to work out why the chairs had been placed as they had in each case.

2 Body posture

The way we *sit* or *stand* conveys our feelings and attitudes.

In groups Volunteers should be asked to sit as if they were:

(i) paying attention,
(ii) bored,
(iii) nervous
(iv) tired,
(v) eager to leave,

and the group should guess which each volunteer chose.

Repeat the exercise with volunteers standing if they were:

(i) hostile,
(ii) ashamed,
(iii) puzzled,
(iv) offended,
(v) suspicious.

Discuss the possible consequences of someone sitting or standing in a way which is not appropriate or not expected eg looking ashamed when someone is merely chatting or bored when someone is trying to interest you.

3 Gestures

Gestures are often used to *emphasize* or *underline* what we're saying.

On your own What sort of things are the people using the gestures below trying to convey to their listener or audience? eg in a) the thumb and forefinger held delicately together could be emphasizing an exact or precise point.

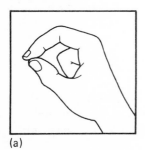
(a)

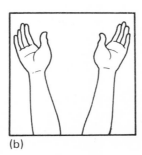
(b)

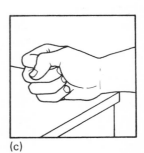
(c)

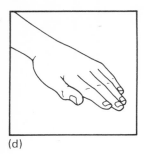 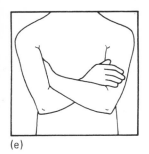

(d)   (e)

As well as emphasizing what we're saying, gestures can *add* to what we're saying or they can give *feedback* to the speaker.

On your own   How would you interpret the following gestures?

(i)   Someone holding their hands up, palm towards you as you're speaking to them.
(ii)   The head being shaken slowly from side to side as someone else is talking.
(iii) The occasional nod by a listener.
(iv)   Someone scratches their head as you're talking to them.
(v)   Frequent nods, one after the other, by a listener.

4   Eye contact

Whether we look at someone and how we look at them in conversations is very important.

On your own   How would you interpret the following?

(i)   Someone looks down continuously as you speak.
(ii)   Someone looks up continuously as you speak.
(iii) Someone you don't know looks at you continuously when you're not having a conversation with them.
(iv)   Someone looks away every time you look at them during a conversation.
(v)   Someone looks at other things in the room as you're talking to them.

In groups   There can be more than one interpretation for each of the above. What more do you need to know about the situation before you can choose one particular interpretation?

5   The face

One of the things mentioned in your group discussion above as something you need to know about in order to interpret a gesture, was probably the sort of expression someone had on their face. Our faces are very subtle indicators of what we think or feel.

On your own The faces below express:
surprise, happiness, sadness, anger, fear. Match the feelings to the
faces.

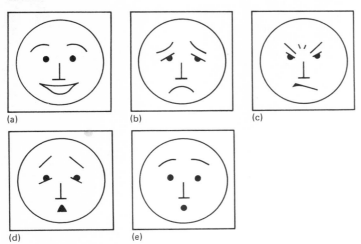

(a)   (b)   (c)

(d)   (e)

We are capable of many varied expressions because of the large number of
muscles which alter the position or shape of our facial features.

In pairs Ask your partner to express the following one after the
other – Anger, puzzlement, no comment, surprise, amazement. Describe
what happens to his/her *eyebrows* as she/he does so.

On your own Try to describe what happens to your *mouth* when you –

(i)   realize you have made a mistake,
(ii) are concentrating,
(iii) are in pain,
(iv) are shocked or surprised.

What makes the human face so expressive are the many possible
combinations of facial features.

On your own Below is a simple drawing of someone smiling happily.

The mouth is clearly turned up and the eyebrows are raised. In the same
way, draw and then describe smiling faces which express:

(i)   joy,
(ii) mischief,
(iii) embarrassment,
(iv) slight disappointment.

11

Unit 2

Elements of speech

When we communicate with someone, we convey our meaning through the words we choose and the order in which we arrange them. But in spoken, as opposed to written, communication, we have additional help conveying our meaning through the *stress, tone, volume, rhythm, pace* and *articulation* of our speech. To misuse these elements can confuse the listener and create misunderstandings.

2.1 Stress

1 Words contain one or more *syllables* or parts of a word. The first five words below contain only one syllable, the second five, more than one syllable.

In groups Say how many syllables each of the second five words has.
   John, word, has, four, five.
   Rescue, believer, communicate, misunderstanding, impossibility.

   In each word of more than one syllable, one or more syllables are more heavily *stressed* or emphasized than others. When we learn how to speak, we learn, at the same time, to say words with the stress or stresses in their natural position in the word.

In groups Pick out the stressed and unstressed syllables in the words below.
explain   syllable
football   confusion
require   pronunciation
office   newspaper
advise   automatically

2 As well as naturally stressing one or more syllables in a word, we may *choose* to stress one word in a sentence rather than another to make our meaning clearer eg. In the sentence 'John ate the apples', I would stress 'John' if I meant it was John rather than Jim who ate them; 'ate' if I wanted to emphasize that John ate them rather than gave them away; and 'apples' if I wanted to say that he ate the apples not the bananas.

On your own Which word in each of the sentences a)–c) would you stress to convey the five meanings (i)–(v)?

13

a) Peter asked you on Thursday if you would phone him today.
(i) Peter not Jane.
(ii) He didn't demand that you do.
(iii) He asked you on Thursday not Friday.
(iv) He asked you not me.
(v) You should phone him today, not tomorrow.

b) Regular customers' invoices have to be prepared tomorrow.
(i) Only the invoices for regular, not occasional customers.
(ii) Their invoices, not their statements of account.
(iii) Tomorrow is the last possible day they can be prepared.
(iv) They should not be sent out tomorrow.
(v) Not yesterday.

c) Are you driving to the party on Saturday?
(i) Will you be doing the driving?
(ii) Are you driving or going by bus?
(iii) As well as driving back from the party.
(iv) Not the disco.
(v) Not on Friday.

2.2 Tone

When someone sings they can sing *high* or *low* notes and the sort of sound their voice makes can be described as *clear, rich, hoarse* and so on. Similarly, the sounds we make when we speak can be high or low and our individual voices can differ in quality.

1 In groups Because it's very difficult to describe our own voices (even if we hear them on tape recordings we don't believe we sound like that!) see if you can describe the quality of the speaking voices of group members.

2 Sound is a good communicator of human *feelings*. Many of us can appreciate the feeling in a piece of music much more directly than that in, say, a poem. Tone is the music of human speech; it is the tone of our voice, rather than the words we choose, which most directly conveys our feelings or attitudes when we speak.

In pairs Say each of the sentences (i)–(v) as if you were:
a) amazed,
b) curious,
c) angry,
d) disapproving,
e) sympathetic.

(i) Hello – when did you get back?
(ii) I've just heard.

(iii) He's going out with her tomorrow.
(iv) You're leaving at the end of the week.
(v) What did you ask me to do?

In groups What did you notice about the *pitch* of your voice (whether it was high or low), when expressing the feelings or attitudes a)–e)? Which other feelings or attitudes are usually expressed by high or low pitch?

3 In **1** we looked at the importance of *stress* in conveying meaning; *tone* is equally important in this respect and is closely related to stress.

In groups Look at the sentences a)–e) in **2**. Choose one of them and repeat the exercise in **2**. How would you describe the *pitch* of the stressed word in relation to that of the other words in the sentence?

In pairs Say the sentences a)–c) below to your partner according to the meaning suggested by the situations (i)–(iii).

a) How long have you been here?
(i) You're late for a meeting with someone and you're apologetic.
(ii) Someone you thought had gone is still waiting and you're surprised to see them.
(iii) You suspect someone of doing something wrong.

b) Could I have a word with you?
(i) Someone's just insulted you.
(ii) You're going to ask someone for a favour.
(iii) You're confused about who someone is.

c) I don't want to do that.
(i) You did it before and it was very unpleasant.
(ii) Someone's insulted you by asking you.
(iii) Someone's been nagging you to do something and you've made it clear that you don't want to do it.

If we use an unexpected or inappropriate tone we can confuse and offend, particularly since people will rely on our tone rather than what we say to judge what we really mean.

In groups Discuss the consequences of saying sentences a)–c) above in an inappropriate tone eg saying a) in situation (i) in the tone appropriate for situation (ii). Do group members recall situations in which they were confused or offended by someone's inappropriate use of tone?

4 We have seen in **2** and **3** that our tone helps to convey our meaning including our feelings and attitudes. But we also use tone to let our listener know what we expect of them. Just as an actor knows when to say or do something when s/he hears or sees another actor saying or doing something, known as an actor's *cue*, so we use tone as a cue, or signal, to our listener to act or say something.

In pairs Say the following a)–c) as if they were the cues indicated in (i)–(iii).

a) Peter.
(i) I want you to come downstairs.
(ii) I want your attention.
(iii) I'd like you to express your opinion.

b) It's Saturday tomorrow.
(i) I don't want to come in to work tomorrow. Will you reconsider?
(ii) This should have been done by tomorrow. When are you going to be able to do it?
(iii) I like Saturdays. How are you going to spend it?

c) I'll see you soon, then.
(i) I'd like to end this conversation quickly.
(ii) I can see you soon, can't I?
(iii) Don't worry about it. I'll have it all worked out by the time I see you.

5 When talking to a group of people, tone is important as a way of *clarifying meaning* for and *having an overall effect* on your audience such as amusing, calming, or emphasizing the seriousness of something.

In groups Radio and TV newsreaders are skilled at using tone as a way of making clear the meaning of what they say. Can you see any common factors in the way different newsreaders use tone? Discuss the tone patterns in their delivery.

In groups Two or three group members should read the passage below, one after the other. The rest of the group should not look at the passage. Then decide which reading made the meaning of the passage most clear. What did tone have to do with this and how was it used to clarify meaning?

Our annual sales figures are a matter of concern. Most areas show a decrease in sales: North Western Area 8% down on last month; Midland Area 10% down; South West 12% and South East – 15%! Although the North-Eastern area did show a small increase, 4%, the overall picture is a gloomy one. Now I know that sales throughout the industry are poor; I know that people aren't very interested in false noses during the Summer, but it is your job to sell them and, in the next few months, which, I hasten to add, are crucial, you must put all your energy into persuading your customers that false noses are the most important items in their stock!

In groups Group members should choose from (i)–(v) below and, without informing the rest of the group of their choice, read the passage again, this time treating it as though:

(i) it were a ghost story,
(ii) it were a joke,
(iii) you were telling someone off,

16

(iv) you were apologising to someone,

(v) you were advertising a product on TV.

How far did the group work out correctly individual member's choices after they'd read the passage? If they did, what did tone have to do with their judgement and if they didn't, how far was incorrect use of tone responsible?

2.3 Volume

The volume expected of our voice depends on the *distance* between speaker and listener and the *nature* of what we are saying. You would not normally shout when talking to a friend in the seat next to you, any more than you would whisper when having heated arguments.

On your own Using a scale of 1–10, where 1 is a very quiet whisper and 10 is a loud shout, write down what you think the appropriate volume would be in the following situations (assume both speaker and listener are in the same room).

(i) Complaining about your service in a shop.

(ii) Giving personal advice to someone while others are in the room.

(iii) Telling someone a secret which you don't want anyone else to hear.

(iv) Chatting with a friend.

(v) Speaking to a group of 30 people in a room.

On your own Using the same scale, suggest what an inappropriate volume in the situations above might be and indicate the possible consequences.

2.4 Rhythm and pace

In **2.1** we looked at how we naturally stress words and syllables and how we can choose to alter our stress according to the meaning we intend. On the whole, we spend longer saying stressed syllables than unstressed syllables. And, using punctuation as our guide, we make shorter or longer pauses between words, phrases and sentences. The way we stress and pause gives *rhythm* to our speech.

On your own Read the passage in **5** and, using a scale of 1–5 where 5 is a long pause and 1 a short one, indicate what length of pause you would use for the following punctuation marks as they appear in the passage.

1.	9.
2:	10;
3;	11,
4;	12,
5–	13,
6!	14,
7,	15,
8,	16,

We have seen that we use *stress* and *tone* to clarify our meaning when reading or speaking. But we may wish to emphasize whole sentences or parts of sentences and, to do this, we can alter the speed or *pace* at which we say them, speaking more slowly for greater emphasis.

In groups Looking again at the passage in **5** decide which are important sentences or parts of sentences and how you would show this by varying your pace.

2.5 Articulation

Each letter of the alphabet is either a *vowel* (a,e,i,o,u) or a *consonant*. On the whole, words tend to have vowels in their middles and end in consonants. (How true is this of the words in the sentence you have just read?) Articulation (the proper sounding of vowels and consonants), if unclear, can lead to ambiguity and misunderstanding.
Major faults are

a) Mumbling – not pronouncing syllables clearly.
b) Failure to sound consonants clearly at the beginnings and ends of words.

On your own If you read the following sentences quickly, you may recognize the faults above.

a) He was unusually impossible, particularly considering the probability of his departure.
b)
(i) Andrew's arch ally, Arthur, asked Adam to answer all enquiries after acting.
(ii) Tina's shoe seems so soft.

In groups Consider the following words or phrases occurring in the passage in **5** and discuss the problems which might arise in their articulation.

(i) annual
(ii) matter
(iii) areas show
(iv) Midland area

18

   (v) show a small increase
  (vi) the overall picture
 (vii) throughout the industry
(viii) very interested
  (ix) which, I hasten to add, are crucial
   (x) most important items

In groups Although clear articulation is important, it must not prevent speech from flowing naturally. Group members should read the passage in **5** paying particular attention to articulation and ensuring that their reading is fluent.

Unit 3

Stating facts – saying what you think

3.1   Stating the facts

1   Messages

In groups   Play a game of Chinese whispers in which one person should think of a short sentence and whisper it to the next person, who whispers it to the next, and so on, until the message reaches the last person who says it out loud. (You can only whisper the message *once*. If you're not sure what you heard, whisper to your neighbour what you *think* you heard.)

The message may have altered by the time it reached the last person. If so, why?

In groups   Repeat the exercise above, but this time use a nonsense sentence such as:

Red apples are dangerous on main roads.
My football had its tea early today.
The fourth day of term sunbathed but didn't take any notice of the Government Health Warning.
Yellow boxes swim quickly if a label is attached to the right big toe of your best friend.
My greatest fear is swallowing a fire engine flashing its bottle of ink in any direction in future, thank you very much.

You may have found that the messages in this exercise changed more than those in the previous exercise. This is because, to retain a message in order to pass it on, we have to *make sense* of it.

In groups   Repeat the two exercises above using longer messages of 2 or 3 sentences.

Again, your messages probably changed more dramatically, because the more *complex* the message, the less easy it becomes to pass it on accurately.

Spoken messages, then, should be stated in such a way that the listener can *understand* the message and should be as *brief* and *simple* as possible.

We can often help the listener by ensuring that our message is composed in a *logical order* which aids memorizing.

21

On your own Write down the following statements in a more simplified way and in a more logical order:

a) 'My results? Yes – er – my results. Right. I got grade 4 in – was it Geography? – no in French – I got a 2 in Geography and English. I got a 2 in English – that's right. Arithmetic was the same as Geography.'

b) 'Go to the Greengrocer's and get 3lb of potatoes and then go to the supermarket – no – the supermarket first because if they haven't got any frozen beans I want fresh ones from the Greengrocer's – and then get an evening paper and – oh – you'd better go to the bread shop first because they might have run out of loaves.'

c) 'If you could take this envelope to Mr. Robson in Marketing – but drop this report into Personnel first – they want it urgently – and you'd better nip over to the Production Manager's Office – I left something there for Mr. Robson – if you could take it to him – and then go for lunch.'

If a message is unclear, it is a good idea to ask questions *at the time* to make sure you have the information you need.

On your own What questions would you ask in the following situations to make sure you had the necessary information?

a) 'Ok then – we'll be arriving at the Station at about 9.30. We'll wait for about ten minutes and then if you don't turn up, make our own way.'

b) 'We'll see you for an interview, then, on Monday afternoon.'

c) 'Mr. Green's not in, you say? Could you ask him to phone me back soon. My name's Hudson.'

d) 'Could you nip to the Stores and get me some nails?'

e) 'Get some chops, butter, bread and eggs.'

2 Making enquiries

One of the difficulties in making enquiries is that you may not be aware of precisely what information you need; and those dealing with enquiries may not be aware of what information you already have and which you require. Both can solve such problems by asking the right questions.

In pairs One of you is a student who has just finished the course described below, and who has been asked to answer queries by people interested in coming on the next course. *Simulate* each enquiry.

a) John – who lives 7 miles away and is worried by travel costs and who wants to work in a shop.

b) Gary, who wants a junior clerical job and hates anything to do with shop work.

c) Elaine, who doesn't like large groups of people and doesn't want to go on the dole after the course finishes.

d) Mandy – whose father could drop her at the college 8.45 am and who is interested in computers.

e) Peter, who would like to learn to type and take some exams in typing. He would also like to improve his Maths and written English.

YOUTH TRAINING SCHEME

Length: 13 weeks
Place: Bursham College of FE

Students will be expected to follow courses in the following:
Office Studies or retailing
Computing/word processing
Communications
Numeracy
Life and Social Skills

Students will attend between 9am and 5pm and will be taught in groups of no more than ten.
A weekly allowance of £25.00 will be paid and travel expenses in excess of £4 will be met.
Of students on the previous YOP course, 40% went straight into jobs, 40% on to 6 month Work Experience placements and 20% onto further courses in the College.

---

3 Instructions

To instruct someone is to tell or show someone how to do something. Often we can show them but when we can't, we have to rely on words, which need to be used *precisely*.

In pairs A should give B directions from college/school/workplace to A's home. Once B receives the directions, s/he should repeat them.

What errors did B make? Was this because B misunderstood the directions or couldn't remember them? Was it because A's directions weren't clear enough?

If someone to whom we're giving directions isn't following us, we may go into greater *detail* ('the road you go down has a post-box on the corner and is opposite a chemist') or try to find landmarks which they *know* ('you know where the Post Office is? Right – now . . . .') The same applies to other sorts of instructions. To ensure understanding we may have to go carefully, in detail, over each step and rely on knowledge the person being instructed already has.

In groups One person with tie-up shoes should put his/her foot on a chair in view of the group. The laces should be untied and then one person in the group should instruct the wearer of the shoe to tie up the laces as if s/he has never done so before. S/he knows the meaning of the word 'loop'.

This exercise was probably more difficult than it appeared to be because tying a shoelace is something we do automatically and don't think about in terms of steps. Our use of language is being severely tested because we are trying to convey to someone totally unfamiliar with something, how to do what to us is very familiar.

On your own Write down instructions for someone to carry out an everyday action as if they've never done it before. The action should be capable of being carried out in the room you are in now, eg opening a window or door; sharpening a pencil; taking off and putting on a sweater; turning on a light.

In pairs Instruct your partner to carry out the action you have chosen.

In groups Each person should choose a game which no-one else in the group knows how to play and then explain the rules of that game.

4 Descriptions

Usually you describe something or someone for the benefit of someone else who hasn't or can't at the moment see what you're describing.

In pairs A should choose someone you both know, either in the group, in or out of College or someone well known, and describe them to B. B should guess who this is. Repeat the exercise.

You probably found that you guessed more quickly if the details given were *precise* ('brown, greasy hair with long sideburns' rather than 'brown hair') and were those details which marked the person off from others ('a tattoo on the arm with a drawing of a ship and 'Gloria' inscribed beneath it').

In groups Each person should choose a household object and describe it to the group as if the group hadn't seen it before.

5 Saying what happened

When reporting an event or sequence of events it is important to say what happened in the order in which it happened. Many events in many situations happen in an order which we expect.

On your own Put the following sequences of events into the order in which you would expect them to happen.

a) Injection – sit in waiting room – ring up for an appointment – ring doorbell – tooth filled – enter waiting room – leave dentist's – make further appointment.
b) Stand up to let someone sit down – get off bus – ring bell for stop – sit down – get on bus – put out hand to stop bus.
c) Dial number – put money in – hear someone answer – lift receiver – hear dialling tone – hear rapid pips – listen to ringing tone – replace receiver.

On your own Write down the order in which you would expect events to happen in the following situations:

a) washing your hair,
b) buying a pair of shoes,
c) boiling an egg,
d) travelling to work/college/school,
e) having lunch.

In pairs A should relate the following sequences of events to B.

a) What you did between last Friday night and Monday morning.
b) What you did this morning between getting up and leaving home.
c) What you have done in the last two hours.
d) Who said what in the most recent conversation you had.
e) What happened at any public event you recently attended eg football match, concert, cinema.

We have been looking at events which happen in a certain expected order. But many events can happen in any order and often it may be important to relate such events in exactly the order they occurred.

On your own In the following reports of events, the reporter is vague about the order in which they occurred. For each, write down two different orders in which the events could have taken place and say why the order of the event is important.

a) 'The two men were walking out of the pub and suddenly both stopped. In no time at all they were punching each other – I'm not sure who attacked whom first – but in the end the short man lay on the floor with the tall man standing over him. Then the police and an ambulance arrived and they were both taken off'.
b) 'I was in the Ladies' Wear department and I know I had my purse then. I'm not sure if I then went to the food hall before the Cosmetics department but I knew it was missing when I left the store.'
c) 'The first car skidded and hit the second one. There was a pedestrian crossing the road, or trying to cross, but I'm not certain whether the first car skidded before the pedestrian stepped onto the road.'

We often disagree about what exactly did happen in a given situation. The same event can be seen from a number of different *points of view*.

On your own   Describe the following events from at least two different points of view. They should be those of people involved in, or witnessing, the incidents.

a)   Someone kicking a ball through a window.
b)   Two young people running quickly along a road.
c)   A man waving from a window.
d)   Two students laughing during a lesson.
e)   Someone leaving a shop in a hurry.

In pairs   Relate to your partner an event which you were recently involved in. S/he should relate the event to you from someone else's point of view.

3.2   Saying what you think

1   Two young people had the following argument.

Martin: I say hang murderers – that's what I say.
Sue: What good will that do?
Martin: Well – they won't be able to murder again, will they?
Sue: They won't be able to murder again if they put them in prison for life.
Martin: But they deserve to die. It's an eye for an eye and a tooth for a tooth.
Sue: So you think everyone should be punished by having done to them what they did to someone else?
Martin: Yeah.
Sue: That just makes us as bad as them, doesn't it?
Martin: They started it – they did it in the first place.
Sue: Anyway – you might be able to do that with murder but what about things like mugging and robbery? You can't rob someone who's just robbed somebody else!
Martin: If you think you're going to be hanged when you kill someone, you'll think twice about it.
Sue: Most murderers don't think about what is going to happen to them when they do it, do they?
Martin: They do.
Sue: They don't.
Martin: Yes, they do.
Sue: No, they don't.
Martin: How do you know?
Sue: It just stands to reason.
Martin: Have you ever murdered someone?

Sue:	No.
Martin:	So you don't know.
Sue:	But since they got rid of the death penalty, murders haven't increased.
Martin:	They have. There's more murders, more violent crime now.
Sue:	Not proportionately.
Martin:	What?
Sue:	Proportionately they haven't increased.
Martin:	Where did you get that from?
Sue:	I read it.
Martin:	Where?
Sue:	I don't know – in the paper.
Martin:	Which paper?
Sue:	I can't remem . . .
Martin:	See – you don't know. You're stupid,
Sue:	So are you.
Martin:	If I'm stupid – how did I get two O levels?
Sue:	You can have two O levels and still be . . .

On your own   Answer the following questions.

a) Sue answers Martin's point that hanging will prevent murderers from murdering again by saying that life imprisonment would do the same. Do you think Sue's point is a good one?

b) Martin then says 'But they deserve to die – ' introducing a new reason to support his view. Would he have done better had he tried to answer Sue's point mentioned in a)? What could he have said?

c) What does 'an eye for an eye and a tooth for a tooth' mean? Does Sue produce a good point against this view?

d) When Sue has made the point mentioned in c) Martin says 'They started it – they did it in the first place.' What does he mean? Do you agree with him?

e) Martin thinks murderers do think about the consequences of their actions before they murder; Sue thinks they don't. Do either of them produce evidence to support their view? What happens to their discussion as a result of this?

2   Answering points

When arguing about an issue, people are often tempted to be more concerned with winning the argument than with listening to another's point of view. As a result, they may try to ignore the other's points and move on to another point of their own. This happens in the argument above when Martin says 'But they deserve to die'. Can you find another place where this happens?

On your own   How would you answer the following points?

a) 'Licensing hours should be kept as they are, otherwise more people will get drunk more often'.
b) 'Young people expect jobs to be more interesting than they are.'
c) 'Motorbikes are so dangerous, they should be banned'.
d) 'TV turns people into morons.'
e) 'You should be able to marry at 16 without your parents' consent'.

In pairs For each of the five statements a)–e) below, see if you can discuss the same point without moving on to another one, for example:

A: We should bring back National Service so that young people learn discipline.
B: National Service won't teach them discipline. You talk to people who did National Service. They didn't learn discipline or anything else which was useful.
A: That doesn't mean that young people today wouldn't benefit from a disciplined life.
B: That depends on what you mean by 'disciplined'. If you mean getting up early and drilling, I'm sure they wouldn't benefit.

a) A: Education should teach you only about what you need to know.
b) A: Corporal punishment should be banned.
c) A: Abortion should be more freely available.
d) A: People in essential services shouldn't strike.
e) A: We should keep our nuclear weapons to make sure no-one else attacks us.

3 Vagueness

People often don't express themselves clearly enough in arguments or discussions. This happened in **1** above when Martin said 'They started it – they did it in the first place.' Part of expressing yourself clearly is ensuring that your listener understands you. She didn't do this when she used the word 'Proportionately'.

On your own Write down one or more of the things which the following statements could mean:

a) 'People in shops don't serve you right'.
b) 'My teachers didn't want to know'.
c) 'My brother's ignorant'.
d) 'John should try harder in class'.
e) 'This film's great'.

4 Logic

If we make a point, we need to support it with good reasons. In the argument in **1** Sue had a number of good reasons to support her view that the death penalty should not be reintroduced – one of which was that it doesn't act as a deterrent since murderers don't think about the consequences of murders before they carry them out.

On your own   Choose the best reasons to support the statements below.

a) There should be less violence on TV because
    (i)   there aren't enough sports programmes.
    (ii) it might have a bad influence on children.
    (iii) my TV's only a black and white one.
b) You should be able to drink in a pub at 16 because
    (i)   17 year olds can get drunk.
    (ii) 16 year olds go into pubs anyway.
    (iii) pubs would sell more beer.
c) There should be tougher laws relating to drinking and driving because
    (i)   drinking damages your health.
    (ii) it is a major cause of road accidents.
    (iii) there are more drivers than there were.
d) Single sex schools are a good idea because
    (i)   girls are cleverer than boys.
    (ii) they produce better exam results than mixed schools.
    (iii) I went to one and was very successful.
e) People should not be able to buy their own council houses because
    (i)   they can't afford it.
    (ii) this makes it more difficult for those presently on council house waiting lists.
    (iii) they're not very good value.

As well as not supporting their arguments with good reasons, people often say one thing which doesn't follow from another.

On your own   Say which of the final statements follow from the two before them. If they don't, what error has been made?

a) London is south of Manchester and Manchester is south of Carlisle *so London is south of Carlisle.*
b) All the people in this group can swim and John is in this group *so John can swim.*
c) Some animals are mammals and a lizard is an animal *so a lizard is a mammal.*
d) Sue is in this group and some of the people in this group can type *so Sue can type.*
e) Some people here can't swim and some people here can't drive *so some people here can't swim or drive.*

Unit 4

Informal talk

4.1 Speech acts

During a conversation, we may perform a series of speech acts: we may ask questions, make requests or suggestions, express agreement, give answers, disagree, object, apologize, and so on. Through our speech acts we *request from* or *convey to* the listener, information, attitudes and feelings. By asking for the time I *request* information, by telling me you *convey* it. Of course, I can request and convey in the same speech act. I can ask you what on earth you are doing with my wallet in your pocket in a way which conveys my disapproval that you have it. And I can convey and request: my telling you that I'm short of cash as we go into the coffee bar is clearly a request for you to pay for my coffee.

1   Questions

'Ask a stupid question . . . .' To obtain the sort of answer you require, you need to be careful about the sort of question you ask.

On your own   Each question below could have produced any of the five answers. But a more carefully worded question would have produced the particular answer given in each case.

Write the questions down.

a) Where do you live?
(i)   I live at 26 Portman Street, Leicester.
(ii)   I live in Leicester.
(iii) I live in the house with the gnome in the garden.
(iv) I live near the main road.
(v)   I live on the Market Estate.
b) What's your name?
(i)   John
(ii)   Smith
(iii) John Algernon Smith
(iv) Algernon
(v)   Smithy
c) What does the job involve?
(i)   You have to work 35 hours per week.
(ii)   You'll be working for Mr. Green.

(iii) Most of the time you'll be filing.

(iv) The post is called 'General Clerical Officer'.

(v) You start at 8–30am and finish at 5pm.

d) What do you think of my work?

(i) You work quite hard.

(ii) You seem suited to the job.

(iii) You seem to enjoy your work.

(iv) You tend to finish tasks as quickly as possible.

(v) You get on well with other staff.

e) To whom should I send this?

(i) Parkinson and Sons

(ii) Mr. Jones

(iii) The Regional Manager

(iv) Mr. R G Jones

(v) The Regional Manager – North West

2 Answers

When giving answers, it is important to know *what sort of answer* is required. Should the answer be long and detailed or brief? Should you give your own views and opinions or not? Should you be plain or tactful?

On your own Which are the most appropriate answers of those given to the questions below? Can you think of a better answer which isn't given?

a) How are you? (Asked by someone to whom you've introduced yourself at the beginning of an interview for a place on a course).

(i) Well – I hurt my knee a couple of weeks ago and it's no better. I must have sprained something down here. Look – I can't put any weight on it . . . .

(ii) Fine thanks. Pleased to meet you.

(iii) I would have been all right if you hadn't kept me waiting for ten minutes.

b) Have you got any brown jumpers in this size? (Asked by a customer in a department store.)

(i) You don't want brown. It'd make you look frumpy.

(ii) No.

(iii) I'm afraid we haven't but we are getting some more in on Friday.

c) What do you think of John? (Asked by the Captain of your football team about to select the team for the next match).

(i) He talks too much.

(ii) He hasn't got the strength of shot we need.

(iii) He's got a car. He'll be able to give us a lift to the match.

d) What qualifications do you have? (Asked at an interview.)

(i) Just a few CSE's.

(ii) 4 CSE's in Arithmetic, French, Science and History – all at Grade2.

(iii) Arithmetic, French, Science and History.

e) Why do you want to work at Carter's? (Asked at an interview.)

(i)   My Dad told me to apply for the job.

(ii) I don't know. I won't until I've started the job, will I?

(iii) The firm's got a good reputation. You offer promotion possibilities and day release. The travelling is all right and the wage seems fair.

3   Putting questions and answers

It is not only important to be careful about asking the right question in order to obtain the sort of answer you want and to be aware of the type of answer required – it is also necessary to think hard about *how you put a question or answer.*

On your own   Which is the most acceptable question or answer below, and why? Can you think of a better alternative?

a) (You lent someone 50p a week ago and they appear to have forgotten.)

(i)   That 50p I lent you – well – I've not forgotten. How about giving it back then?

(ii) I'll have that 50p back, if you don't mind.

(iii) Do you remember that 50p I lent you? I'm sure you've forgotten but do you think I could have it back?

b) (A friend starts to cry in front of you.)

(i)   Come on then – are you going to tell me all about it?

(ii) What are you crying about then?

(iii) Do you want to talk about what's upset you?

c) (You ask your supervisor if you can leave work half an hour early).

(i)   It will be OK if I leave work half an hour early on Friday, won't it?

(ii) What would you say to my leaving work half an hour early on Friday?

(iii) Would it be possible for me to leave work half an hour early on Friday?

d) (A boy asks his girlfriend if she wants to carry on going out with him.)

(i)   No.

(ii) I don't think its a good idea for us to go on seeing each other.

(iii) I don't like you anymore.

e) (Your supervisor asks you why you're late.)

(i)   I don't know really. I just am, that's all.

(ii) I'm afraid I missed my usual bus.

(iii) Buses.

4   Simulations

We rarely perform speech acts in isolation but more often in conversations and conversational exchanges.

In pairs   Simulate the situations below, each of which requires a series of speech acts.

In groups   After each set of simulations a), b) and c) discuss the questions at the end of **4**.

a) *Bad news*
(i)   Boyfriend A tells girlfriend B he wants to break off their engagement.
(ii)   Friend A comes into school/college to tell B his motorbike has been stolen.
(iii) A has borrowed friend B's pocket calculator and seems to have broken it.
(iv)   A tells friend B that a close friend of theirs has had an accident and is in hospital.

b) *Conveying attitudes*
(i)   A's friend B has upset a mutual friend. C and A disapproves. S/he tells B.
(ii)   B has made a mistake at work which A has discovered. A tells B.
(iii) A states an opinion which B disagrees with.
(iv)   Foreman A at work asks B to do a job which B doesn't think s/he ought to do.

c) *Conveying feelings*
(i)   A, a close friend of B, has said something about him/her in conversation with a group of friends which has hurt B. A and B are left alone afterwards.
(ii)   Friend A has broken a promise to B which makes him/her very angry.
(iii) Friend B has got the impression that A doesn't like him/her. They are talking.
(iv)   B has just returned to college/work after one of his/her parents has died. A has coffee with B.

Questions

1   How direct or indirect was the speaker in each case? eg 'Hey – your bike's been stolen!' rather than 'I've got some bad news for you . . .'
2   How important was it for the speaker to adopt an appropriate attitude to what s/he had to say? eg laughter and giggles before 'Guess what – I've broken your calculator!'.
3   How far was the speaker's knowledge of the listener's attitude or feeling important in determining how s/he put what s/he had to say? eg finding out about someone's emotional state before giving them bad news. Was any attempt made to find out early in the exchange, if it wasn't already known? eg 'Look – this can wait until later if you like . . .'
4   Did speaker or listener anticipate what would be said to them? eg 'Look – I don't think you're going to like what I've got to say' or 'Listen – if it's bad news – don't mince words – tell me straight'.
5   How did the relationship between speaker and listener affect how the speaker put what s/he had to say? Consider:

a)   The status of each. (Teacher/pupil/   Employer/employee Friend/ friend.)

b) How A sees B. (I like him/her.)
c) How A thinks B sees him/her. (S/he likes me.)
d) A's view of what B thinks in the way A sees B. (S/he thinks I like him/her.)

4.2 Conversations

1 Holding conversations

Most of the conversational exchanges we have possess a clear purpose. However, many conversations may have no such clear purpose but are held to pass the time, for enjoyment or to get to know someone. In fact, some people consider the ability to hold a conversation an important quality in a person. There are no rules governing effective conversation but the following points are worth considering:

a) *Breaking the ice*
Starting a conversation is often the most difficult part of it. A statement or question which relaxes people, puts them at their ease can be the best way to begin. Try to think of something both partners have in common, eg when waiting for an interview you might ask another interviewee 'Are you as nervous as I am?' or 'What's the interviewer like?'
b) Try to work out what topic of conversation your partner might be interested in, eg it might not be productive to ask an elderly relative which band s/he likes.
c) Ask questions rather than sit there waiting to be asked them.
d) Make sure any questions you ask are likely to be ones your partner is prepared to answer.
e) Be sensitive to your partner's willingness to engage in conversation. There are times when we aren't keen to talk to anyone.

In pairs Bearing a)–e) above in mind, *simulate* the following.
(i) Two young people are waiting to be interviewed for a job.
(ii) You and a friend, A, meet A's friend C whom you have never met. A leaves the room for a time.
(iii) You are looking after a friend of your parents until they arrive home.

In pairs Hold a conversation for 5 minutes about topics which interest you.

2 Conversations

On your own For each of two or three conversations you have recently had, answer the following questions:
1 What stances or positions did participants take? (See Unit 1.)
2 Do you remember any looks or gestures which provided feedback? (See

Unit 1.)
3 What was the purpose(s) of the conversation? (To pass the time, convey information, get someone to do something?)
4 Did one person dominate the conversation? Why was this?
5 How would you describe the spoken style of the participants – formal/informal? angry/excited tones? cool, carefully stated sentences? (See Unit 2 'Elements of speech'.)
6 Were you disappointed with your performance during the conversation? Was there any way in which you could have improved it?

4.3   Conflicts and misunderstandings

In Unit 1 we saw that conflicts and misunderstandings often arose because of stereotyping, and misinterpretation of non-verbal gestures and feedback. Conflicts and misunderstandings may also arise from the following.

1   Jumping to conclusions

On your own   After each of the following, the speaker could be going to say a number of things and it is possible to jump to a number of conclusions. What are they?

a) (Supervisor at work) 'About your work – I've had my eye on you for some time and there's something you ought to know . . . .'
b) (Parent) 'You know you washed the dishes yesterday . . . .'
c) (Friend) 'Is that the blouse you bought last week . . . .?'
d) (Friend) 'How much money have you got on you?'
e) (Fellow worker) 'Have those invoices been sent off yet?'

In pairs   Simulate the above exchanges.

2   Assuming wrongly that a particular relationship exists between speaker and listener

On your own   In the following, what sort of relationship did the speaker assume existed and what relationship is indicated by the person making the reply?

a) S: I believe you're having problems at home. If you are, I'm sure . . .
     R: I don't think that's your business really.
b) S: Cover for me while I nip out to the shops.
     R: I'm sorry – I'm not prepared to do that Mr. Jones.
c) S: How's that old heap of metal you're driving?
     R: If you mean my car – it's running very well, thank you.
d) S: How are things, Lurch?
     R: The name's Darren.
     S: Sorry – how are things, Darren?

e) S: Sir – could I give you that piece of work tomorrow?
   R: Don't call me that. It's Mr. Robinson or Peter.

3 Communicating information to the inappropriate person

On your own What could have caused offence in the following situations and whom do you consider responsible?

a) Supervisor A comments to employee B about the standard of the work of employee C who is of the same status. B tells C.
b) A tells B that C has asked her out and she has refused. B lets C know s/he knows.
c) A tells B and not C that s/he is not going to C's party to which s/he's been invited.
d) A learns from colleague B that his/her application for promotion has been turned down by C.
e) Employee C tells supervisor B that Head of Section A has told him/her to do X and not Y which supervisor B has told him/her to do.

4 Differing opinions or attitudes

In pairs Simulate the following.

a) A and B think friend C has stolen something. A wants to forget it but B doesn't.
b) Your mother or father wants you to do an educational course. You don't.
c) Your girlfriend wants you to go to a party at her friend's. You don't want to go.
d) A work mate thinks you should do a job in a particular way. You disagree.
e) Your supervisor considers your work slapdash. You think it's acceptable.

5 Two people possessing different information about a situation

In pairs Simulate the following:

a) Friend A has heard that B has been spreading rumours about him/her. B knows s/he hasn't.
b) Your brother/sister tells your parents that you have been mistreating him/her. One of your parents confronts you.
c) You arrange to meet a friend at 7.30 pm. You think the meeting time was 8.30 pm. and when you turn up s/he is still waiting.
d) Supervisor A asks you to do a job in the morning. Supervisor B then tells you the same job can wait until the afternoon and you do what s/he says. You meet supervisor A at lunchtime.
e) Employee A tells fellow employee B that employee C is getting paid more than B for the same job but C is receiving the same. B confronts C.

Unit 5

Formal talk

5.1 Formal/informal

Unit 4 concentrated on talk in *informal* situations; this unit will look at talk in *formal* situations – with which you are likely to be less familiar. Firstly, what are the differences between formal and informal situations? As we shall see, certain situations can be seen as formal or informal, depending on the decisions of those involved (consider the interviewer who says 'Now just relax – this is going to be very informal'). However, we can pick out some general differences.

1 Rules

We abide by rules in both sorts of situations but, on the whole, the rules we follow in formal situations are *clearer*. For example, the rules governing the procedure of meetings of most organizations are written down and an agenda is drawn up. People are expected to obey the rule of not talking about Item 3 on the agenda until Item 2 has been discussed. Imagine meeting a girlfriend or boyfriend with an agenda of items to be discussed by you during your night out!

On your own Below is a series of rules. Some of these tend to be followed in formal situations, others in informal situations. State which are which and, for each, give an example of a situation in which it might be followed.

a) Greeting someone by kissing them.
b) Finishing what you have to say by proposing a toast.
c) Introducing people by their first names.
d) Sitting very close while talking.
e) Standing up straight while talking.
f) Only speaking when asked a question.
g) Sitting back in a relaxed way.
h) Introducing someone as Mr./Mrs./Miss./Ms. and their surnames.
i) Greeting by shaking hands.
j) Introducing yourself and telling someone the purpose of your visit.

2 Spoken style

The situation we are in makes a certain *style of speech* appropriate.

On your own   Each of the following phrases is used either in an informal or formal situation.
State which and then write down how you would say the same thing in the opposite type of situation – formal or informal.

a)   I'm pleased to be able to welcome you here tonight.
b)   You're joking!
c)   Could you tell me your name please?
d)   Shall we adjourn for lunch?
e)   I'd be grateful if you would be seated.
f)   We will be letting you know as soon as possible.
g)   Fancy a coffee?
h)   How are things?
i)   I would like to support the view of the previous speaker, Mr. Green.
j)   Isn't he back yet?

3   Public and private

On the whole, formal talk tends to take place in *public* situations with a *larger number of people* present whom you *don't know very well,* whereas informal talk often occurs in *private* situations with a *smaller number of people* present whom you tend to *know well.*

On your own   Would you expect the following to be said in formal or in informal situations and approximately how many people would you expect to be present?

a)   Mr Peters – are you busy? I have quite a long queue here.
b)   See you later.
c)   I love you.
d)   Doreen – where's the carbon paper?
e)   John and I want to thank you for all the presents we've received.
f)   Could we move on to Item 2 – the Treasurer's Report?
g)   Have you any experience relevant to the job?
h)   Pass that stapler, mate.
i)   Don't you be late in the morning, son.
j)   I was walking down Mayfield Avenue at 10 pm on Thursday 20th November, when I noticed a young man on a motorcycle steering erratically.

5.2   Dealing with people in formal situations

We saw in **5.1** that we tend to follow certain rules and speak in an appropriate way in formal situations. We expect to be treated in particular ways in such situations and, if we are not, the result can be misunderstanding and communication breakdown.

1 Proper address

One way in which people expect to be treated is by being *addressed* in the appropriate way.

On your own   What would you expect to be called by the following?

a) A fellow sales assistant referring to you when speaking to a customer.
b) A personnel officer interviewing you for a job.
c) A waiter in a restaurant.
d) Someone serving you in a shop.
e) Your supervisor in front of a group of fellow workers/students.

What would you call?

a) Someone your own age whom you're serving in a shop.
b) Your boss/supervisor when talking in private to a friend.
c) Your boss/supervisor when talking to them.
d) Someone waiting at your receptionist desk whom you are announcing over the phone to the person they have come to see.
e) A customer standing in front of you and to whom you're referring when talking to another sales assistant?

In groups   Discuss the differences between people's answers. Is there anything more you needed to know about some of the situations in order to be clear about the appropriate style of address?
Discuss the possible consequences of an in appropriate style of address in the situations above.

2 Situation

Susan and Mark work on Saturdays in Johnsons Electrical Shop. It is 1 pm and the manager, Mr. Thompson, is at lunch. A customer, Mr. Richmond, comes in and walks up to the counter. Susan and Mark are sitting behind the counter, talking and eating cakes.

Susan	(*to Mark*) It's all right when Thompson disappears for $1\frac{1}{2}$ hours, isn't it?
Mark	It's nearly 2 hours now.
Susan	But when we're five minutes late he loses his bottle.
Mr. Richmond	Excuse me.
Mark	(*to Susan*) And he expects you to stay late, doesn't he?
Susan	I'm going to ask for extra pay if he tries that again.
Mr. Richmond	Excuse me.
Mark	(*Mouth still full of cake and still seated*) Won't be a minute. (*to Susan*) . . . . or just refuse. That's what I'm going to do if he asks me again. He's got no right. (*to Mr. Richmond – getting up.*) Yeah?
Mr. Richmond	Do you sell international adaptors?

Mark	(*screwing his face up and raising his eyebrows as if totally bewildered.*) Ey?
Mr. Richmond	International adaptors – do you sell them?
Mark	(*to Susan*) International . . . (*to Mr. Richmond*) . . . what?
Mr. Richmond	Adaptors.
Mark	(*to Susan*) This bloke wants international adaptors.
Mr. Richmond	I only want one.
Mark	(*to Susan*) Do we do them?
Susan	Don't ask me.
Mark	(*to Mr. Richmond*) What are they when they're at home then?
Mr. Richmond	They're adaptors so that you can use electrical appliances abroad. I'm going on holiday next week.
Mark	Where are you going?
Mr. Richmond	Italy actually.
Mark	My sister went there last year. Rimini. She didn't like it. This hotel she stayed in . . .
Mr. Richmond	Look – do you sell them or don't you?
Mark	(*looking at Mr. Richmond angrily and raising his eyes to Susan*) I'll have a look.
Mr. Richmond	Never mind.
Mark	Come back this afternoon when Thompson's here – he'll know.
Mr. Richmond	(*leaving*) I don't think I'll bother.
Mark	Suit yourself.
	(*Mr. Richmond exits*)
Mark	What was up with him then?
Susan	Not a clue.

What do you think 'was up' with Mr. Richmond?
Mark and Susan could be criticized for the way they dealt with him, in particular with regard to *body posture, facial gesture, style of address, style of speech and irrelevant remarks*.

On your own Write down the points you would criticize Mark and Susan for and say why.

In groups Discuss your conclusions.

5.3 The interview

Jane applied for the job advertised opposite and was interviewed by Mr. Grant.

TRAVEL COMPANY
requires
Bright school leaver
16 or 17 with good shorthand/
typing and good English to
join them in their High St.
office.

Ability to deal with the public
an advantage.

Hours 9 – 5-30 5 weeks holiday
£3000 + L.V's. Cheap Travel.
Apply Mr. Grant 262 – 1422.

Mr. Grant shows Jane into his office and sits behind a desk. Jane sits clutching her handbag on her knee with her head down, only raising it when she speaks.

MR. GRANT Now then Jane, tell me something about yourself.
JANE Well, I . . . . . er . . . . I live in Bilston and . . . . . er . . . . I went to Well Park School, which I just left. Not just – I mean I left . . . . when did I leave? I left, you know, in the Summer. I've applied for quite a few jobs without much luck. And . . . . . I think that's all there is really.
MR. GRANT What about School? Which subjects did you like? Which did you do well at?
JANE Biology was all right. And Art. But we mucked about a lot in the 5th year. And we kept having different teachers. It was all right though, I suppose.
MR. GRANT What were your exam passes?
JANE I can't remember. Wait a minute – English, Arithmetic, Geography, European Studies – all Grade 3 or 4. And then there was Typing R.S.A. Stage I . . . . which I failed but I think I should have passed really. I got some more but I can't remember.
MR. GRANT Why do you think you're suited for this job?
JANE Well . . . . I fancy the idea of working in a Travel Company. A friend of my mother does and she gets cheap travel and she's going to be a courier now. I just think it'd be a good place to work.
MR. GRANT If you got the job, how difficult would the travelling be?
JANE I'm not sure – my Mum brought me this morning. (*she giggles*)
MR. GRANT Right Jane. Have you any questions to ask me?

JANE	Er . . . . . . er . . . . . yes – the pay – what would it be?
MR. GRANT	£3000 a year to start with – but that was in the advert wasn't it?
JANE	How much is that per week?
MR. GRANT	It's about £60. (*pause*) No more questions? (*pause*) Thanks very much for coming. We'll be letting you know in a couple of days' time.

Below are some of the criticisms made by interviewers about applicants for jobs.

On your own Read through them and tick off those you think apply to Jane's interview with Mr. Grant.

a) Inappropriate non-verbal communication.
b) Unable to talk about self.
c) Hadn't prepared answers to likely questions.
d) Misunderstanding questions asked.
e) Answers couldn't be heard clearly.
f) Vague rambling answers rather than clear and concise ones.
g) Irrelevant answers.
h) Not thinking about implications of answers.
i) Apparent lack of interest in job and interview.
j) Unsuitable for the job but not aware of this.
k) Inappropriate style of speech – use of slang, colloquialisms.
l) No knowledge of the nature of the organization.
m) Lack of confidence.
n) Unrealistic overconfidence.
o) Not steering the interview to their advantage.
p) Repeating points already made.
q) No questions to ask interviewer.

On your own Compose a job advertisement similar to the one above.

In pairs Using the same questions Mr. Grant put to Jane, interview each other for the job in your advert. Then tick off any error listed above which you and your interviewer think you made.

5.4 Meetings

Meetings are held for a variety of reasons, three of the more common being to *debate an issue*, to *reach a decision about action* and to *produce ideas*. They can range in nature from the most formal board meeting to a discussion between friends.

In groups of 4 or 5 Decide whether your meeting is going to debate, reach a decision or produce ideas. Select a topic from those given below (if you can't find a suitable one, choose your own) and then elect a chairperson. Decide on a rough time limit. Record the meeting on tape if you can.

Topics to debate

a) Nuclear disarmament
b) Censorship
c) Juvenile crime and its treatment
d) Drug abuse and drug control
e) Capital punishment
f) Abortion
g) Youth unemployment
h) The role of the police in society
i) Industrial action
j) The ages at which you are permitted to do different things such as marry, drink, vote and so on

Decisions to reach (For each of these topics, it will be necessary to add your own details to the situation before beginning the meeting.)

a) The local authority has three empty Victorian houses which it wishes the community to use. Work out who would use the houses and what priority you would give different people or groups.
b) You suspect someone in the group to be regularly stealing money and valuables from you. Decide what to do about it.
c) A friend in the group has had a very upsetting experience. S/he disappears after lunch after telling one group member s/he was thinking of committing suicide. Work out what you would do.
d) One person in the group says s/he has been threatened by a crowd of girls/boys who have said they are going to wait for her/him after college. Consider different courses of action and their advantages/disadvantages.
e) You are at College/School/Work and are told that a nuclear bomb is going to fall ten miles away in 2 hours' time. Decide what you would do.

Subjects to produce ideas about

a) Items for a half-hour radio programme for young people, organized by your group.
b) As many uses as possible for an empty matchbox.
c) You have been asked to re-organize the course you're following for next year's students.
d) Invent a new ball game.
e) Decide on a theme for a friend's 18th birthday disco and think up competitions you could organize to liven up the evening.
f) A very severe winter is expected. Draw up a list of precautions people could take to help them during the bad weather.
g) Find the best name for a new band specializing in 60's Soul music and Reggae.
h) Draw up a list of local sights and places of interest for a new tourist

guide to your area.

i) The local authority is to provide purpose-built accommodation for young single people. They ask you for advice about the sort of housing which would be suitable.

j) Unusual ways of raising money for a local charity.

On your own After your meeting has finished, write down those qualities of a good chairperson or good participant, chosen from the list below, which you think you displayed.

In groups Now read out your comments to the rest of the group and see if they agree or not. If you recorded the meeting, play it back – this might resolve any disagreements which arise.

Qualities of a good chairperson

a) Able to ensure participants state points clearly.
b) Doesn't dominate discussion.
c) If participants disagree – able to make clear the conflicting points to others.
d) Able to summarize the discussion so far.
e) Can sum up the mood or view of the majority of participants.
f) Has a clear idea of ground not yet covered.
g) When discussion is not productive, steers it in a more stimulating direction.
h) Able to control dominant speakers and encourage reluctant ones.
i) Can keep in mind the purpose of the meeting.

Qualities of a good participant

a) Puts forward ideas briefly and clearly.
b) Listens to others and ensures s/he understands what they mean.
c) Disagrees without causing offence.
d) Tries not to dominate the discussion.
e) Is prepared to defend own opinions – not just accept the views of others weakly and uncritically.
f) Contributes relevant points and doesn't divert the meeting from important issues.
g) Does not restrict the meeting to a conflict between himself/herself and another participant.

5.5 Speaking to a group of people

1 Usually, when people are asked to speak to a group, they have time to plan what they are going to say and how they are going to say it. However, occasions may arise when we may have to speak at short notice. On such occasions we have to be able to think 'on our feet'.

In groups

a) A teacher or group member should choose a topic from the list below and give it to a group member who should talk about it immediately for 30 seconds, fluently and with only brief pauses.

Paper	Trousers
Socks	Salt
Wednesdays	Plastic
Number 11	Names
Metal	Tables

b) This time, topics chosen from the list below should be given to group members who have 5 minutes to prepare what they are going to say before talking for a further 2 minutes. This speech should interest the audience and have some sort of order and sense.

Money	Holidays
The sea	Music
Films	Cars
Animals	Friends
Fashion	Hair

2 Giving a speech to a group of people is an ordeal. Almost everyone finds difficulty standing up with confidence and delivering a speech without being affected by nerves. Often speaking to a small number of people who know you is more difficult than speaking to a large group who don't know you. However, *preparing* what you are going to say beforehand helps and, as with many things, *practice* improves performance.

Below is some advice which might help you prepare and give a speech.

Preparing a speech

a) Choose a topic which *interests* you. It is far harder to interest an audience in something which you have no interest in.

b) Make *notes* for your speech. Writing every word down may make you feel more secure before you give the speech, but this can lead to a stale, monotonous presentation and prevent you maintaining eye contact during your speech. (See i) below.) Your notes should state clearly your *main points* and contain sub-headings indicating briefly what you're going to say in connection with each main point.

c) Making notes ensures your speech will have a *logical order* in which one point follows from another. This will help your audience follow, digest and remember what you say.

d) Try to find out what your *audience is likely to know* about your topic. This will prevent you telling them what they already know or using technical terms which they don't understand.

Giving a speech

e) Make sure you are standing in a *comfortable* position, that you can see all your audience and they can see you. (Often a table is useful for resting notes on and can provide a barrier which makes you feel more secure.)

f) Good speakers present their material in a *fresh, novel* way. Make sure you are not just giving a list of facts. Vary your content: information as well as personal anecdotes and examples. Begin in an unusual way which captures your audience's interest: end in a way which leaves them with something to think about.

g) Visual aids such as charts, diagrams, objects often add to your speech.

h) Make sure your voice has the correct volume, that you articulate clearly and vary your tone. (See Unit 2 'Elements of speech'.)

i) Remember Non-Verbal Communication. Don't look down at your notes too often because you will break *eye contact* and lose your audience's attention. Try to maintain eye contact regularly with 2 or 3 people chosen from different parts of your audience. Try not to *turn your back* on your audience if using a chart or a blackboard. Make sure you use hands in *illustrative gestures* and vary your *facial expression*. Try to control distracting gestures such as holding your hand in front of your face, nail-biting, lip-chewing, note-rustling, head-scratching.

On your own Give a speech lasting 5–10 minutes on a topic which interests you. This should be followed by a short period when your audience can ask you questions.

Unit 6

Using the phone

6.1 To call or not to call

Before looking at how we use the telephone, we should consider when we would *choose* the phone rather than other forms of communication.

On your own In each of the situations below, decide whether you would use the phone or some other form of communication.
Give reasons for your choice.

a) You see a newspaper advertisement for a job, inviting people to send for application forms.
b) A close friend's father dies and you want to express your sympathy to him/her.
c) You want to tell your girlfriend/boyfriend you don't want to see them any longer.
d) You're going to a party and want to invite friends you don't see daily.
e) You work as a clerk in a Sales Department and one of your representatives has asked you to book him into a hotel at the weekend. It is now Wednesday.
f) You smell gas at home and decide to inform the Gas Board.
g) You buy something, take it home and discover it's faulty.
h) You leave your bag, containing important possessions, on the bus.
i) You are asked to arrange a meeting of ten members of staff and need to find out when they are available.
j) You have now decided on a time for the meeting in i) and need to inform the ten members of the staff about it.

In groups Discuss your individual decisions, particularly when there was disagreement. What are the main reasons for preferring the phone call?

6.2 Speaking on the phone

Speaking on the phone is very different from speaking to someone face-to-face. On the phone, you do not have the help of the *non-verbal communication* we looked at in Unit 1.

In pairs With your eyes closed or (if tempted to peep) back to back, simulate a situation in which A should tell B something B will not like.

In groups Discuss what difficulties arose in this exercise as a result of neither partner being able to see the other.

Any difficulties discussed probably arose from A & B's inability to use non-verbal communication to *add to, emphasize* and *clarify* what they were saying or to give to or obtain from the other partner, *feedback* about what was being said.

Without non-verbal communication we rely entirely on those *elements of speech* we looked at in Unit 2: stress, tone, volume, rhythm, pace and articulation.

When making a phone call, it is the following points which are particularly important to remember:

- **Stress** Stress we saw was helpful in *clarifying* meaning and *emphasizing* certain words. Before making a phone call, pick out *key words* or ideas you might stress.
- **Tone** Tone is vitally important in the absence of non-verbal communication. Tone, more than anything, is responsible for speakers jumping to conclusions about the attitudes and feelings of others.
- **Volume** Make sure you can be heard. Politely inform the caller if you cannot hear him/her, particularly when there is interference on the line.
- **Rhythm and pace** Are you speaking too quickly, particularly if someone is trying to take down your message? Don't be too quick to interrupt when the caller pauses: it is more difficult to know when it is your turn to speak on the phone than in a face-to-face situation.
- **Articulation** Are you sounding syllables of potentially difficult words clearly? If in doubt, spell out the word.

6.3   Preparing to make a call

If the call is not straight forward:

a) *Make notes* for your call. Write down the points you wish to make, the questions you want to ask, the answers to questions which might be put to you.

b) Make sure you have the *information* you're likely to need – figures, reference books, diagrams – so that you don't have to leave the phone during the call.

c) Have a *pencil* and *paper* by the phone.

In pairs Make notes for the following calls – A for calls (i) and (ii) B for calls (iii) and (iv).

(i) You phone up about a job in the newspaper 'Wanted soon – Junior for busy office – 061–163–4114'.

(ii) Your favourite band is playing locally and you wish to book tickets for yourself and three friends. You can only go together on Wednesday or Thursday. The advertisement reads 'Lyceum – Mon Tue Wed Thur 'Favourite Band' plus support '2nd Favourite Band,' Tickets £2.50, £3.50, £4.00'.

(iii) You ring your local college about courses in Business Studies.

(iv) You receive a phone message from a friend who's thinking of applying for the course you're on at the moment. S/he wants you to phone him/her back to let him/her know all about it.

When you've made your notes *simulate* the calls. Before doing so, however, A and B should work out (and where appropriate, invent) the information they think the caller will require when they are receivers – A for calls (iii) and (iv), B for calls (i) and (ii).

6.4   The phone call

1   Beginning the call

When *making* a formal telephone call you should:
(i)   State your name and, when appropriate, that of your department or firm.
(ii)   State the name of the person you wish to speak to.
(iii) Indicate the purpose of your call.

When *receiving* a formal telephone call you should:

(i)   Greet the caller (Good Morning/Good Afternoon).
(ii)   State the name of your department or firm.
(iii) Ask if you can help the caller.
(iv)   If the caller wishes to be put through to an extension, say 'I'm connecting you now'. If the extension is engaged, 'Would you like to hold?' If the caller does hold, a reassuring 'The line is still engaged' or 'I'm trying to connect you', is suitable.
(v)   Remember that first impressions are important. You may be representing your department or organization.
(iv)   Try not to get flustered. Calmly follow (i)–(iv) above.

On your own   What, if anything, is wrong with the openings of the telephone calls below?
(i)   A: Good morning – Aldersons Plumbing Supplies.
       B: I bought a bath from you yesterday – remember?
(ii)   A: Hello.
       B: Is that Aldersons?
       A: That's right.
(iii) A: Good morning. I'm enquiring about the job you advertised. I'm not sure if you have to phone up or fill in an application form, so I thought I'd give you a ring anyway. I've had quite a lot of selling experience and I'm sure I'd be suitable.

B: Excuse me sir. I don't think we have advertised any vacancies recently.

A: This is Aldersons, isn't it?

B: I'm afraid you have the wrong number. This is J T Taylor & Sons.

(iv) A: Hello – could you give me Sales?

B: Who would you like to speak to Sir? There are five extensions.

(v) A: Hello – is that Aldersons?

B: Yes – who's that?

In groups Discuss your findings. Who was responsible for what went wrong in each case?

2 During the call

a) *Spoken style*

In Unit 4, we saw that the situation we are in makes a certain style of speech appropriate and that in formal situations, when speaking to someone we don't know very well, a formal spoken style is expected. Many phone calls in a work situation are of this type.

On your own The following informal phrases were used in formal calls. Try to say the same thing in a more formal style.

(i)   Hang on – I'll get a pen.

(ii)   Steady on – you're talking too quickly.

(iii)   I didn't catch that – come again.

(iv)   Speak up.

(v)   You'll just have to phone back later – he's not in.

(vi)   Cool down. You're getting all worked up.

(vii)   The line's engaged. You'll have to wait.

(viii) She's not in right now. I'll do, won't I?

(ix)   I'm much too busy – you'll have to wait.

(x)   She's got you the wrong extension, mate. It's 29 you want.

b) *Messages*

In Unit 3 we saw how easily the meaning of spoken messages can be changed as they are passed on. To ensure the accurate relaying of phone messages, the following points should be noted:

When *leaving* a message:

(i) In **6.3** it was suggested you make notes for all but the most straight-forward calls. The further advantage of doing this is that if the person you wish to speak to is not available you have a message for them clearly set out in written form. This is particularly valuable if you have to leave a recorded message. Ensure you read out your message in a *logical* order to help the receiver of the message.

(ii) State clearly what *action* you require from the person for whom the message is being left when s/he receives it. Should they ring back? If so, when?

52

(iii) If the receiver doesn't do so, ask him/her to *read back* the message to you after you've given it to them, to ensure it has been taken down accurately.

When *receiving* a message:

(i) Most message pads have headings for this information but, if one isn't to hand, ensure you have the following details: date, time, name and phone number of the caller, what action is required, your name as receiver of the message.

(ii) Make sure you *understand* the message as you're taking it down. Ask *questions* if you're unsure.

(iii) If a message is not given in a *logical order* – try to put it in order before you write out the final message.

(iv) *Read back* the message to check you've recorded it accurately.

In pairs Bearing the above points in mind, *simulate* the following calls taking it in turns to be message *leaver* and *receiver*.

(i) L: Your name is Peter Robinson and you work for Pitts (Tel: 051-114-4695) a firm supplying engineering parts. You have had an order from Mr. Green at Walfords but you are out of stock of the following parts specified in his order – 4B 56, 4A 57, 5C 124, 6R 995, 7L 423, 8B 561, 9U 429. You ring Walfords to see if they wish to order alternative parts.

R: You are Mary Nelson. You work as a stock records clerk at Walfords – a medium heavy engineering firm. You receive a call for your colleague Mr. Green, who is out of the office. It is 3.20 pm 4th March.

(ii) L: Your name is Mr/s Lewis and you have taken several options on holidays at Travel-Wise your local travel agents. You ring up to confirm the holiday you have finally chosen: Torremolinos, Spain at the Hotel Minorca for 14 nights from the 14th – 28th August, Tour 423, flying from Birmingham. You want full board and a private bathroom. Your phone number is 021-100-1442.

R: Your name is Sally Gray and you work at Travel-Wise, a travel agents. Your colleague Lucy Davis has been dealing with Mr/s Lewis, a client was has options on several holidays. It is 10.30 am 10th April.

(iii) L: You are Mr. Roper and your wife works at Timpson's a small shop in the High Street. You have arranged to meet in the High Street at 5.30 pm but you can't make it until 6.30. pm. If your wife can't meet you, could she ring you back in her lunch hour on 142-9981 Ext. 4339? Otherwise you will assume she can meet you.

R: You are Mrs. Davidson, manageress of Timpson's, a small shop in the High Street. You have a phone call for one of your staff, Mrs. Roper, who is serving a customer at that time.

(iv) L: You are Mr. Stokes, the Service Manager of Cooper's Garages Ltd.

A Ford Escort has been brought in for a 6,000 mile service by a Mrs. Peters. You have found a small hole in the exhaust. It is not dangerous, but the exhaust will have to be replaced fairly soon. You ring Mrs. Peters and leave a message for her to ring you within two hours to let you know whether to replace the exhaust.

R: Your name is Alice Parker and you work in the typing pool at Harrisons. There is a phone call for your colleague Rosemary Peters who is having her coffee break. You are leaving soon for the dentist's and won't be back at work until tomorrow. The call is made at 10.30 am June 15th.

(v) L: You are Linda Alan and you are secretary to the Headteacher of Furley Primary School. A pupil, John Hawkins, has hurt his foot in a gym lesson. It seems like a sprain but one of the teachers has taken him to the Casualty Department at St Peter's Hospital, Wharton Road to have an X-ray. You phone his father.

R: You are Peter Thompson. There is a phone call for your colleague Peter Hawkins but he is out. It is 3.15 pm, 2nd July.

c) *Making an appointment*

When making an appointment by phone you should make sure before you dial that you know:

(i) what you are making it for;
(ii) when you want it (and what other times and days are suitable if your first choice is not available);
(iii) whom you wish to see.

The table below tells you which doctors in group practice are present during a surgery and who is out on his/her rounds at which times on a particular day. Patients can see any doctor, but the doctors insist that they should only make home calls if the patient cannot get to the surgery.

Doctor	Morning surgery	Afternoon surgery	Evening surgery
	9 a.m.–11 a.m.	2 p.m.–4 p.m.	6 p.m.–8 p.m.
SMITH	IN	OUT ON ROUNDS	OFF DUTY
ROBINSON	OFF DUTY	IN	IN
KHAN	IN	IN	OUT ON ROUNDS
MIDDLETON	OUT ON ROUNDS	IN	IN
SIO WHA	IN	OUT ON ROUNDS	IN

In pairs Simulate the following phone calls made by patients to the surgery between 8 am and 9 am, A taking the role of the patient, B the surgery receptionist. B should note the appointment time and, in the cases of house calls, the nature of the illness. Surgery appointments are made at ten minute intervals. House calls cannot be made at a specific time.

(i) David Roberts has hurt his arm. It is uncomfortable but he is not in agony. He can only come in the evening and usually sees Dr. Smith or Dr. Robinson. Time of call 8 am.

(ii) Mrs Childs rings on behalf of her bedridden mother. There is a sudden rise in her temperature. She usually sees Dr. Khan or Dr. Middleton. Time of call 8.20 am.

(iii) Alan Jones has no energy, feels tired and listless. He can come morning or afternoon and would prefer to see Dr. Sio Wha. Time of call 8.30 am.

(iv) Mrs. Cathour rings on behalf of her 5 year old son, Michael. He is vomiting continually. Time of call 8.35 am.

(v) Helen Milne has a bad cough and tight chest. She can only come in the morning and would prefer to see Dr. Sio Wha. Could she be seen before 9.30 am? Time of call 8.50 am.

d) *Dealing with a problem*

Problem phone calls are best dealt with if a sensible *approach* is taken to handling them in the first place.

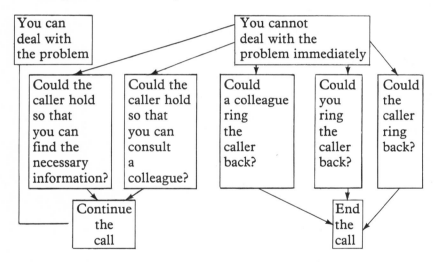

On your own Using the diagram above, decide what course of action you would choose when receiving the call below. (You may choose a course of action not shown on the diagram.)

(i) During your first day at work in a salaries department, a disgruntled ex-employee rings up with a complex enquiry about holiday pay s/he hasn't received. You are alone in the office for 20 minutes.

(ii) You work at a travel agents. A client calls wanting to know whether her tickets have arrived. You are serving a customer, there is a queue and the files are at the other end of the shop.

(iii) You work as a sales assistant in the furniture department of a large store. A call is put through to you complaining about a non-delivery of a three-piece suite. The despatch department has details of delivery arrangements.

(iv) On your first day in a large office, the phone rings for Mr. Green. You don't know if he works in your office or not.

(v) You work in a mail order firm. A customer phones up complaining that goods s/he ordered have not arrived. S/he claims to have already spoken to your colleague (at present busy on another phone) who said his/her goods would arrive today.

Problem calls are often based on *misunderstandings*.

On your own What has gone wrong in the following calls?

(i)   A: Ah – yes – now – you're the gentleman with the leaking roof. Well I can tell you . . .
      B: There's nothing wrong with my roof.

(ii) A: I didn't ring because I thought you said you were going to call me back.
      B: I didn't ring for the same reason.

(iii) A: What do you mean 'Could you pass the file?'! What file?
      B: Sorry sir – I was talking to a colleague.

(iv) A: Well love, I should think . . .
      B: A bit less of the 'love', thank you very much!

(v)   A: No – I'm interested in buying a TV, not renting one.
      B: Oh – I'm sorry. I thought you said . . .

Many problem calls are the result of *angry* or *ineffective* callers.

In pairs The following phrases were used by callers at one point during a conversation. Work out between you what the situation could be, who used the phrase and at what point it was used, then *simulate* the call.

(i)   I want to speak to someone higher up, this minute!

(ii) What I want to know about it is – What's it – sort of – you know – how . . . . . er . . . .

(iii) Are you trying to give me the run around?

(iv) Are you the idiot I was talking to the other day?

(v)   I am not losing my temper. I am angry with good reason.

6.5   Be like that . . .

Peter Lawson works at Clarks Travel Ltd, a coach firm, in Thornton. He takes bookings and does general clerical work. Peter receives a call from Mr. Farrington, Head of the Geography Department at Thornton Comprehensive.

Peter   Hello? What can I do you for?
Mr. F   This is Clark's, isn't it?
Peter   Clark's Travel. Who else?
Mr. F   Who am I speaking to?

Peter	Oh – Mr. Lawson here.
Mr. F	You were the gentleman I was speaking to last time, weren't you? I'm Mr. Farrington, Thornton Comprehensive.
Peter	Barrington, Barrington. Doesn't ring a bell, mate.
Mr. F	No – Farrington.
Peter	That's what I said.
Mr. F	Farrington. With an 'F'.
Peter	Oh – Farrington. No – can't recall, I'm afraid. Anyhow – what's your problem?
Mr. F	I haven't got a problem. I'd like to alter a booking arrangement I made with you, if I can.
Peter	Hang on a minute. (*Peter leaves the phone for a few moments, then returns.*) Now then – what were you saying?
Mr. F	I booked a coach with you two weeks ago.
Peter	Oh yes – Cornwall.
Mr. F	No – Yorkshire.
Peter	Yorkshire? I'm sure it was Cornwall. Oh – now I remember – Heathfield Comprehensive.
Mr. F	No – Thornton Comprehensive.
Peter	Hang about – I'll get your file. (*Peter leaves the phone for a few moments, then returns.*) Now then. Mr. Farrington – Thornton Comprehensive. . . . (*The next few words can't be heard.*)
Mr. F	I'm sorry – I didn't quite hear that.
Peter	(*Irritated*) I said 'Malham Cove – Yorkshire'!
Mr. F	Yes – that's right. I previously had a party of 25 but it's now 45. So I'd like a 45 seater please.
Peter	Was 45 – now you want 25. Well you're out of luck – I don't think we have any 25 seaters free.
Mr. F	No – it was 25 and now I want a 45 seater.
Peter	Oh – I see. I can't manage it.
Mr. F	Why not?
Peter	I'm sorry. I wasn't talking to you. I was talking to my mate. He wanted me to go for a coffee break. Well – I don't know if we can do a 45 seater.
Mr. F	When can you let me know definitely?
Peter	Dunno really. Only Handley knows that.
Mr. F	Who's he?
Peter	He's the manager, isn't he?
Mr. F	Yes – well is he there?
Peter	No – he's out today.
Mr. F	Should I phone tomorrow then?
Peter	You could.
Mr. F	Actually – I won't bother. I need an answer on this fairly quickly. I'd like to cancel our booking. I'm going to try some other firms.
Peter	Be like that. We don't need the work, you know. (*Mr. Farrington puts the receiver down*) Snowed under we are pal, more than we can cope with. We can do without your . . . hello . . . hello.

In groups Discuss the ways in which Peter handled the phone call badly.

Unit 7

Persuasion and negotiation

7.1 Persuasion

1 Points of view

In Unit 3, we saw that everyday events could be seen from different *points of view*. A person waving from a window might be drunk, choking from fumes, trying to attract attention, waving someone goodbye. But, as well as events, ideas, objects and situations can be seen from different points of view. When we are persuading, we are trying to get others to accept such a point of view.

On your own The statements below present a *negative* point of view. Rewrite them in such a way that they present a *positive* point of view. (Eg a negative way of describing half a bottle of milk is to say it is 'half empty'; a positive description would be 'half full'.)

a) We could lose this match 3–1 if they manage to get another.
b) It's my twentieth birthday on Thursday. I'm ancient!
c) They only had brown cord jeans left. Hundreds and hundreds, in all sorts of styles and sizes – but all the same colour.
d) It's another hour before we go home.
e) I have to start work at the crack of dawn every day – 8.30 am!

2 Skills

In everday life we often use and are the objects of persuasion skills. Before looking at some everyday situations, assess your persuasion skills and your ability to resist persuasion, in the situations below.

In pairs One partner should attempt to persuade the other, who should, at the time, attempt to resist persuasion.

a) Choose a number from 1–20 and persuade your partner that it is the most important number of all.
b) Try to get your partner to let you sit in his/her chair.
c) There is something outside the window your partner should see.
d) Persuade your partner to agree that your favourite band, song, a type of music is the best.
e) Try to get your partner to sing a song.

In pairs Simulate the following everyday situations, after having invented the details you will need to know.

a) A is trying to persuade B to let C, a mutual friend, go along with them on a night out. B doesn't want C to go along.

b) B tries to persuade employer A that s/he is worth a pay rise. A is not so sure.

c) A wants to go on holiday with his/her girlfriend/boyfriend. Parent B is against the idea.

d) A is going to thump friend C for insulting him/her. B tries to prevent A doing so.

e) B refuses to give a talk to the rest of his/her school/college group. A tries to persuade him/her to do so.

3 Emotive language

As we shall see in **4**, advertisers persuade us by using words to create a particular *impression, feeling,* or *emotion*. Some words are more suited than others to create or express such emotions. For example, to describe the behaviour of a group of young people as resulting from high spirits, is to express and invite feelings of tolerance towards them; to describe it as 'rowdy' invites and expresses intolerance and disapproval.

On your own The table below contains a series of emotive or non-emotive descriptions. Try to find the equivalent of each description.

	Emotive	Non-emotive
a)	?	Young people
b)	Nuclear holocaust	?
c)	?	Withdrawal of labour
d)	Getting the sack	?
e)	Social security scroungers	?
f)	?	Civil unrest
g)	Do gooders	?
h)	?	Neutralize enemy positions

4 Advertisement

Look at the following advertisement.

```
WANTED

Young, enthusiastic Person
Friday for Dynamic Public
Relations Outfit. Join a
lively, trendy team in this
new, go-getting firm. If
you want a job where talent
counts – ring Susie –
061–125–1234.
```

On your way to the phone box to ring about the job, you meet a school-friend of yours. It turns out that s/he has just given up the job you are about to apply for. This is what s/he says.

'I handed my notice in after a month. "Person Friday?" That's a laugh. "Person-every-day-of-the-week" mate, that's what I was. I did all the rubbish jobs – the one's no-one else wanted to do. And I don't know what they mean by "young". Not one of them was a day under 30. "Go-getting firm" did they say? Well, they went and got a 3 hour lunch every day. The only talent you'll use is knowing who doesn't take sugar in their tea'.

Your friend has given you a different picture of the very job which seemed so attractive in the advert.

On your own Either choose a suitable advert from a newspaper, or make up your own and then write down a very different version of what the job might be like.

By the skilful use of language as well as music and images, advertisers try to persuade us to buy a product, attracting us because of our desires and needs.

In groups Pick out the particular words or phrases in the job advert above which you find attractive/persuasive. Do they build up a clear impression of the job in your mind?

In small groups Invent a product, give it a name, discuss its selling points (the features which you want to emphasize to make the product attractive) and then devise a 30 second radio advert to be broadcast on your local commercial radio station. (Record it if a cassette recorder is available).

In groups Present your adverts to the rest of the group.

5 Sales talk

When you are next in a market or large store, listen carefully to the market trader or to a demonstrator selling a product. To persuade you to buy, they may stress the following points:

(i) The usefulness of the product.
(ii) The product's cheapness considering its value.
(iii) There are only a few still available for sale.
(iv) You personally are going to receive a bargain.

In groups Group members should each choose an everday object, such as a pencil, ruler, bag etc. Using the points (i)–(iv) above, they should spend 5 minutes preparing a demonstration of the object and are then allowed one minute, during which they should try to sell as many of their objects as possible to the group, who should imagine they haven't seen any of these objects before.

Whether you are working in a department store, travelling, selling door-to-door, it is likely that the organization for which you work will have some form of sales training. This is often accompanied by a sales manual giving you practical guidance about how to conduct a sale. Here is the last page of such a manual.

DON'T FORGET

1 Always be *courteous* and *polite*.
   The customer is *always right*.
2 *Know your product*. Be ready
   to answer any questions.
3 Be *positive* about the product.
   Emphasize its *benefits* to the
   customer.
4 *Know your customer*. Why are they
   buying? How interested
   are they?
5 Don't *hurry* or *put pressure* on
   the customer. Don't force a sale.

In pairs Together, invent a product and a situation in which it would be sold. (You may wish to use the product from **4**.) One partner should be the sales person, the other the customer. The sales person should ensure s/he has a grasp of point **2** above. The customer should work out why s/he is interested in the product, how interested s/he is and work out questions s/he wishes to ask. Now *simulate* the situation.

In groups In the light of the simulations, discuss whether any points should be added to the ones in the sales manual above and whether any of the points should be altered.

7.2 Negotiation

Whether with their families or friends, in work, college or school, people, as individuals and groups, have differing needs, desires, beliefs and interests and it is often necessary to *negotiate* an agreement about a situation or course of action which satisfies all parties.

1 Persuasion

Negotiation involves *persuasion*, in so far as your point of view or case needs to be presented as powerfully and attractively as possible.

On your own Look back over **7.1** and, in the light of what you have learned, spend 10 minutes preparing a case for or against one of the issues below. Then present your case in no more than 2 minutes. If none of the issues below appeals to you, choose your own.

a) The value of vocational preparation courses for young people.
b) Changing the age at which people are allowed to drink alcohol in pubs.
c) The compulsory wearing of crash helmets and/or seatbelts.
d) Home taping of records.
e) Proposals to lessen the strain on prisons by giving fewer and shorter prison sentences.

2 Agreement

If you are persuading, you are concerned that someone accepts your point of view. Negotiation, although it involves persuasion, also requires that you come to an *agreement*. In doing so, it is necessary to be positive and to find *common ground* between you.

In pairs You have 30 seconds to reach agreement in each of the following situations.

a) You are going to buy a record or cassette between you. Decide which.
b) The two of you are asked to choose somewhere close by for a group visit.
c) Find 3 TV programmes you both enjoy.
d) Choose a subject which is part of your course you both would like to spend more time on.
e) Select a name for a band you are both members of.

The exercise above was relatively straightforward. Most negotiating is more complex and it is hard to find common ground because of the difficulty of seeing the situation from the other's point of view.

On your own Try to describe briefly how the people below might see and feel about the situations they are in.

a) The occupant of a house, outside which young people congregate every night.
b) A teacher, whose students are not interested in what s/he's teaching.
c) A neighbour who complains that your stereo is too loud.

d) A parent, whose son/daughter does not return from a night out.
e) An employer who is told by an employee that the job s/he is doing is boring.

3

One of the most difficult decisions when negotiating is when to *assert yourself* and *stand your own ground* and when to *compromise*.

On your own In the following situations, decide what you would do, and write down what alternative courses of action there might be.

a) You buy a watch. After a week, you realise it is faulty. You feel entitled to an immediate replacement but the shop assistant will only offer to send it away to be repaired.
b) A friend borrows £5 from you and promises to give it back by Friday. Friday comes but your friend apologises saying s/he can't afford to repay you and could you wait until the following Friday.
c) A teacher asks you to leave the room for something you didn't do.
d) An employer tells you at interview that there will be a wide variety of work for you to do. After 2 months you have only done one or two repetitive jobs.
e) A shop assistant is rude to you after you complain about the service s/he has given you.

In groups Compare your answers. Where it was difficult to decide on a course of action. What more did you need to know about the situation to help you make a decision?

Assignments 1–3

Assignments 1

South Thames Insurance Brokers

South Thames Insurance Brokers is a subsidiary of the South Albion Insurance Group. South Thames has four High Street shop/offices in the South London suburbs. The New Green shop is managed by Mr. Foster, who is in his mid-30's. He believes in training 'on the job' and encourages you, Alan Davis – a school-leaver who's just started with the firm, to ask questions if you're not certain about anything. Ann Rossiter, 18, also works full-time as a clerk/typist. South Thames specializes in motor insurance but does do a small amount of other types of insurance.

1A   A new quote

If someone wants to take out a motor insurance policy, they tend to phone different brokers and compare quotations. The premium (the sum payable annually required to maintain the policy) is calculated taking a series of factors into account: if a car is kept in a garage, it is considered to be a lower risk than if it is kept on the road outside the home; under 25 drivers are considered higher risks than drivers aged over 25, and so on. When you give a phone quotation, you find out all the information listed on the New Quote sheet and then, using the points system, calculate the premium.

In pairs   Task 1

In your first week, you are shown a New Quote sheet and ask Ann Rossiter to explain the factors you don't understand.
Simulate the explanation.

	New quote	
MAKE	NCB	
MODEL	USE	
CC	GARAGE	YES/NO
YEAR	WHERE BORN	
VALUE	PHYS DEF	
COVER	FULL PROVIS	
IOD	AGE	
I&S	OCC	
ALD	ACC	
U25 YES/NO	CONVIC	
EXCESS	COY	
AREA		

	New Quote		
MAKE	The car manufacturer -Ford, Honda, VW etc.	**NCB**	Do you have a No Claims Bonus? **
MODEL	Saloon, Sports etc.	**USE**	SDP Comm Trav etc ***
CC	Cubic capacity of the engine 1200, 1300, 1600 etc.	**GARAGE**	Will the car be kept in one?
YEAR	-of manufacture	**WHERE BORN**	Town and Country of birth
VALUE	Current market value	**PHYS DEF**	Any physical deformities or infirmities?
* **COVER**	Type of insurance cover TP/TPFT/COMP	**FULL PROVIS**	Type of driving Licence
IOD	Only the insured will be covered for driving	**AGE**	–
I&S	Insured and spouse will be covered	**OCC**	Occupation
ALD	Any licensed driver will be covered	**ACC**	Have you ever had a motor accident?
U 25 **YES/NO**	Will any of the drivers covered be under 25?	**CONVIC**	Do you have any convictions for motor offences?
EXCESS	Do you wish to pay an excess? (The first portion of the cost of any claim.)	**COY**	company or Companies giving the quotation
AREA	The area the car will be used in		

* TP – Third Party – this covers only liabilities to passengers, pedestrians.
TPFT – Third Party, Fire and Theft – Third party cover plus cover for fire damage to/theft of your vehicle.
COMP – Comprehensive – TP, TPET plus (usually) damage to your own car, windscreen breakage, medical expenses, theft of personal belongings from your vehicle.
** A No Claims Bonus is an amount deducted from your premium if you haven't made a claim for a particular period.
*** SDP – Social, Domestic and Pleasure Use.
Comm Trav – Use for commercial travelling. Other business uses.

In pairs   Task 2

Mr. Bates phones up to ask for a quote. Alan should use the New Quote Sheet as a checklist and **simulate** the conversation with Mr. Bates, calculating the premium and giving him a quote for a Celtic insurance policy.

Premium Calculation – Celtic Insurance		
		Points
MODEL	SALOON CONVERTIBLE SPORTS	+ 10 + 15 + 20
CC	OVER 1600 1300–1600 UNDER 1300	+ 20 + 15 + 10
YEAR	1980 & LATER 1975 – 1979 1970 – 1974 1965 – 1969 BEFORE	+ 10 + 15 + 20 + 25 + 30
COVER	TPO TPFT COMP	+ 10 + 20 + 40
DRIVER(S)	IOD I & S ALD U 25	+ 10 + 20 + 30 + 40
EXCESS	1st £50 1st £25	− 20 − 10
* AREA *** NEW GREEN AREA – B**	A B C D	+ 10 + 15 + 20 + 30
USE	SDP COMM. TRAV. OTHER COMM. USE.	+ 10 + 20 + 30
GARAGE	IN GARAGE PARTLY COVERED IN OPEN	+ 10 + 15 + 20
FULL/PROV	FULL PROV.	+ 10 + 30
AGE	17–18 19–25 25–30 30–40 40–60 OVER 60	+ 40 + 40 + 20 + 15 + 10 + 40

For Make, NCB, Where Born, Phys. Def., OCC, ACC, CONVIC – refer to insurance company.

Points	Premium
280–300	£250
260–280	£230
240–260	£210
220–240	£190
210–220	£170
200–210	£150
180–200	£130
160–180	£110
140–160	£ 90
120–140	£ 70
100–120	£ 60
80– 10	£ 50

Information for Mr. Bates
You are a chartered accountant who has just passed your test and this is your first insurance policy. You own a 1973 VW Beetle 1300cc saloon. You want only to insure yourself. You are 33 years of age. You wish to pay an excess of £25. You have a garage and only wish to use the car for social, domestic and pleasure purposes. You are perfectly healthy, with no accidents or convictions. You want comprehensive cover.

On your own   Task 3

Mr. Bates is pleased with the figure you give him and you send him a proposal form. One morning you receive a recorded telephone message. 'Mr. Bates here. I'd still like the policy but I've now got a new car, a VW Beetle 1200 1975. I'd like to insure my wife (she's 26 years of age) as well as myself but, apart from that, everything else remains the same. Oh – I don't want to pay anything now'.
  Draft a letter to Mr. Bates, giving a second quote on the basis of the new information and requesting clarification of anything unclear in the message.
Your address: 123 High Street, New Green, London, SE7.
Mr. Bates: 14 Moorside Lane, New Green.

In pairs   Task 4

Mr. Bates receives your letter and phones you. **Simulate** the conversation and give him a third quote on the basis of the information you receive.
Information for Mr. Bates
By 'I don't want to pay anything now', you meant you didn't want to pay any excess.

1B The accident report form

When a client has a motor accident you send them a report form to fill in. This has to be completed in the fullest detail, otherwise the claim might be invalid. You receive such a report form from Mr. Norton which you consider has been incorrectly completed.

On your own   Task 1

Read the form and **make notes** for a phone call to Mr. Norton, detailing exactly what is wrong with the form.

In pairs   Task 2

You ring Mr. Norton. You know from experience that clients who have made errors often feel embarrassed and occasionally become aggressive – so make sure you are tactful. **Simulate** the conversation.

General Insurance Company

ACCIDENT CLAIM FORM

FULL NAME: *James Alexander Norton*
ADDRESS: *52 Ivy Close, New Green*   PHONE NO: *New Green 4626*
POLICY NO: *H 225 63914*
VEHICLE *Mine*   REG.NO: *UKV 424 P*

DETAILS OF ACCIDENT

Date *Thursday*   Time *7.30*   Place *New Green*
Who was driving? *Me*
Details of other persons or vehicles involved   *No – one*
Name and addresses of witnesses (if any)
Road conditions at the time   *Quite nice*
Damage to vehicle   *Front's done in*
Brief details of what happened. (Include a sketch map if this will help).   *Went into a lamp post.*

In pairs   Task 3

Mr. Norton comes into the shop. You help him to **complete the form.**
Information for Mr. Norton.
Your broker, Mr. Davis, will probably need the following information:

a)   The accident took place in Dean Way, New Green.
b)   It occurred at 7–30 in the morning.
c)   It occurred on Thursday 24th July, 1982.
d)   The front nearside wheel arch was dented and the wheel buckled.

e) You were driving down Dean Way. Near the junction with Colliers Close, a dog ran out of a house on the right. You braked and swerved to the left to avoid it. You mounted the pavement and hit the lamp-post nearest the junction.

f) It was a fine, clear, dry morning. Road conditions very good.

g) Your car is a Ford Fiesta.

1C   A claim

A client, Mr. Whitley, who has a home and family policy, requests a claim form. He was camping with his family when a fire destroyed their tent and some personal belongings. He returns the claim form below.

After looking carefully at a description of the policy (below) you realize Mr Whitley will not be entitled to the sum claimed.

SECTION 1V
Please specify goods lost or damaged with estimated replacement cost.

ITEM	COST
1 Nikon Camera	£120
1 Pair Binoculars	£200
cash	£100
Contact Lenses	£150
1 cassette Recorder	£45
Jewellery	£180
Rubber Dingy	£80
Camping Gas stove	£95
Tent	£200
TOTAL	£ <u>1170</u>

On your own   Task 1

Calculate the amount Mr. Whitley is entitled to. (Remember to deduct the excess of £10 for the claim.)

ALL RISKS

Loss or damage by ANY CAUSE happening to any of the following. You select which you wish to cover:–

NOTE – The *MINIMUM* sum acceptable for cover under Item A is £1,000.

A: PERSONAL EFFECTS & CLOTHING; JEWELLERY, GOLD & SILVER ARTICLES, SIMILAR VALUABLES, FURS; LEISURE EQUIPMENT (i.e. cameras and their equipment, projectors, binoculars and other optical equipment, tape and cassette recorders (all for private and amateur use) portable TV's, radios, record players and the like); SPORTS EQUIPMENT & ANCILLARY CLOTHING.
Miscellaneous unspecified items of the above up to £250 any one article, pair or set. Items valued in excess of £250 should be described in the Proposal.

B: PERSONAL MONEY – up to £200 any one loss & CREDIT or CASH DISPENSER CARDS (i.e. fraudulent use by a finder of a lost card) – up to £200 any one loss.

C: PEDAL CYCLES any number unspecified up to £250 any one loss. Cycles valued in excess of £250 should be described in the Proposal.

Excess: £10 all claims for Items A and B and specified articles of Leisure or Sports Equipment.
£10 all accidental damage claims for C.

All the above property is covered whilst anywhere in the UK, Continent of Europe (except Albania, Czechoslovakia, East Germany, USSR) Mediterranean coast and islands, Madeira, Canary Islands, and Azores (and during journeys by recognised sea and air routes between these territories).

NOT COVERED:
(i) contact or corneal lenses, hearing aids;
(ii) wear, tear, deterioration, moth, mildew, vermin, atmospheric conditions, action of light;
(iii) any process of dyeing, cleaning, repairing or restoring;
(iv) mechanical or electrical breakdown or derangement of any equipment or by its misuse, or repair, adjustment or interference with any component part;
(v) errors, omissions, depreciation in connection with Money;
(vi) cycles used for racing, pacemaking, speed trials;
(vii) riot and civil commotion outside Great Britain or requisition of any article by customs or other authorised bodies;
(viii) loss or damage to Sports Equipment whilst in actual use;
(ix) loss or damage to camping equipment, animals, vehicles, watercraft.

VALUATIONS: We require sight of these for any item of jewellery, similar valuables or furs valued at £500 or above.

On your own   Task 2

Make notes for a phone call to Mr. Whitley. You will send the claim in as it is but need to inform him that he will not receive the sum originally claimed.

On your own   Task 3

Mr. Whitley is out when you call. **Record a message** on his machine.

Assignments 2

Travel Well Ltd

Travel Well Ltd have a chain of five agencies in the Southern Suburbs of Lanchester, an East Midlands City. The Barton Shop, situated in a busy high street, is managed by Gwen Roper, a woman in her early 40's who has worked for the firm for ten years. Before that she was a tour representative in the Mediterranean and she knows the travel business well. There is a full-time typist, Louise, who works in the office at the back and four full-time assistants behind the counter: they include Anne, the assistant manager, who is in her late 20's and wants to be a tour representative and John, 23, who used to work in a bank but found promotion slow.

2A   Hoverover Ltd

You are Susan Archwell, a school-leaver who has just joined the Barton branch of Travel Well Ltd. Gwen Roper informs you that, for the first month, she only wants you to handle straightforward rail, coach, air and hovercraft/ferry bookings. The shop has a recorded message service and, each morning, you have to listen to the messages and select the ones you think you can deal with. One of these is the message below.

'Yes – this is Mr Naylor, 5 Beech Court, Barton. My wife, myself and my 2 children want to take a hovercraft from Dover to Calais on Monday July 16th. We'd be able to get down to Dover by about 10–30 am so a flight round about that time would be fine. My number is, 625–1432. If you could ring me back and let me know if you can make a booking'.

John helps you find the correct page in the Prestel information service relating to flights by Hoverover from Dover to Calais. The table opposite appears on your screen.

John explains that X means the flight is fully booked; – means there is no flight at that time; R that you should ring Hoverover to check availability; and A that you can take a booking without having to check availability.

On your own   Task 1

Write notes for your return call to Mr. Naylor, including any questions you wish to ask him.

74

	M	T	W	T	F	S	S	M	T	W	T	F	S	S
HOVEROVER flight availability JULY 9 – 22														
Flight time	9	10	11	12	13	14	15	16	17	18	19	20	21	22
502 0630	X	R	R	A	X	R	A	X	X	X	R	A	X	R
503 0730	X	X	R	X	–	–	–	X	X	R	R	A	X	R
504 0830	X	X	R	X	–	X	R	X	R	X	–	–	–	–
505 0930	A	A	R	R	–	R	R	A	A	X	R	X	X	R
506 1030	A	A	R	X	–	–	X	A	R	X	–	–	X	R
507 1130	X	R	R	A	–	A	X	A	A	R	A	X	R	A
508 1230	X	X	R	R	R	R	A	R	X	A	–	–	–	R

Cost	Single	Day return	Period return
ADULT	£12.00	£14.00	£18.00
CHILD 14–16		10% REDUCTION	
12–14		20% "	
8–12		40% "	
UNDER 8		50% "	

In pairs   Task 2

Simulate the call to Mr. Naylor.

Information for Mr. Naylor:
1 You would like to know the total cost of the fares.
2 You want period returns.
3 Your children are aged 5 and 7.

In pairs   Task 3

Mr. Naylor comes into the shop later in the day to make his booking.
Simulate the encounter.

Information for Mr. Naylor:
You have decided:
1 not to take the children;
2 to go a week earlier at the same time.

On your own   Task 4

Overleaf is the ticket you issue to Mr. Naylor. Either copy it and
complete it, or **write down** the information you would complete it with.

```
┌─────────────────────────────────────────────────────────┐
│                    TRAVEL WELL LTD                       │
│                                                         │
│      Head Office: 14 Grant Street, Lanchester 525–1321  │
│                                                         │
│   Operator:              From:                          │
│   Flight No:                                            │
│   Time:                  Destination:                   │
│   Date of Travel:                                       │
│   Passenger(s):                                         │
│                                                         │
│   Received the sum of £   :      from                   │
│                                                         │
│   Date                           Issued by              │
│                                                         │
└─────────────────────────────────────────────────────────┘
```

2B   Jewels of the North

Susan has been with Travel Well Ltd for 6 months and is now doing a wider range of work. Mr. Wallace, an elderly gentleman who is very hard of hearing, comes into the shop one day and wants to book a coach tour. Mrs. Roper has always advised that when dealing with the elderly or the hard of hearing, staff should speak particularly clearly and write all details down for the client to take away with them. Mr. Wallace is keen on a coach tour of Scotland and you choose the one opposite for him.

Additional information: Deposit £11.50 (Includes £3.50 insurance additional to holiday cost). Balance must be received 8 weeks or more prior to holiday departure. Pick up at Northampton, Grosvenor Centre Bus Station, Greyfriars. 12.30 pm.

In pairs   Task 1

Mr. Wallace is shortsighted and hasn't brought his glasses with him. **Describe** the holiday to him, using the information above.

In threes   Task 2

Mr. Wallace is keen on the holiday. You **phone** the tour operator to take out an option on it (this means the holiday is reserved for 24 hours).
Information for Mr. Wallace
Your first choice is the June 6 tour, your second the July 4. You would like to join at Northampton.

Departures: Mondays: weekly May 23 to Sept 5 inc. For departure points and times see page 4.

Visiting:– Yorkshire Dales, Cumbria, Scottish Lowlands and Highlands, Loch Lomond, Loch Long, Oban, Caledonian Canal, Inverness, Wick, John O' Groats, Kyle of Tongue, Reay, Dornoch Firth, Speyside, Royal Deeside, St. Andrews, Edinburgh.

Your tour day by day
DAY 1 – LEEDS
Leaving London we travel to Bedford and Northampton and then to Oakham and Melton Mowbray, Ollerton and Blyth to Leeds for overnight at the Golden Lion Hotel. (Tel. 0532 36454).

DAY 2 – OBAN
We make our way through the Yorkshire Dales to Skipton and Settle and into Cumbria to join the motorway to Gretna Green then through the Border Country to Erskine Bridge and Loch Lomond, Arrochar, Inveraray and Loch Awe to Oban. Overnight at the Columba Hotel. (Tel. 0631 2377).

DAY 3 – FORT WILLIAM
Morning at leisure and luncheon in Oban. We then depart for Fort William following Loch Creran to Portnacroish and Loch Linnhe to Ballachulish and Fort William. Overnight at The Croit Anna Hotel. (Tel. 0397 2926).

DAY 4 – WICK
We travel the length of the Caledonian Canal via Loch Lochy, Glen More and by the shores of Loch Ness to Inverness. We cross the new Kessock Bridge to the Black Isle and Evanton. Thence to Bonar Bridge, Lairg, by Loch Loyal to Tongue, Melvich, Thurso and Watten to arrive in Wick for a two night stay at the Station Hotel. (Tel. 0955 3452).

DAY 5 – WICK
Morning at leisure to explore this ancient Royal Burgh and fishing port with its interesting harbour and the Caithness Glass Factory. In the afternoon we take a drive to John O' Groats, Dunnet Bay and Castletown.

DAY 6 – BALLATER
We travel along the Caithness coastal road through Dunbeath, Helmsdale and Golspie to Bonar Bridge, then by the Cromarty Firth to Dingwall and Inverness. From Carrbridge we enter Speyside and continue our journey to Royal Deeside via Tomintoul. We arrive in Ballater for a two night stay at the Loirston Hotel. (Tel. 033 82 413).

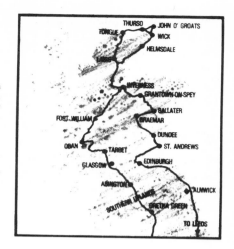

DAY 7 – BALLATER
At leisure to explore this attractive Highland village.

DAY 8 – EDINBURGH
Our journey takes us to Braemar and through Glenshee to Blairgowrie and Dundee then over the Tay Bridge into Fife. We pass through St. Andrews and over the Forth Bridge to Edinburgh for an overnight stay at Green's Hotel. (Tel. 031 337 6311).

DAY 9 – LEEDS
We have the morning at leisure in Edinburgh for sightseeing or shopping and after taking an early luncheon at Green's Hotel we travel south on the Great North Road through Northumbria and into Yorkshire to Wetherby. Thence to Leeds for overnight at the Metropole Hotel. (Tel. 0532 450841).

DAY 10 – HOME
We have the morning at leisure in Leeds, taking lunch at the Metropole Hotel. We then travel south to return to our original point of departure.

REAL VALUE FOR MONEY PRICES

HOL. 274 MAIN SEASON		10 DAYS		MONDAYS
May 23, 30	June 6, 13, 20, 27	July 4, 11, 18, 25	Aug. 1, 8, 15, 22, 29	Sept. 5
£245	£245	£245	£245	£245
FULL	FULL	PLACES	PLACES	PLACES

You require the following details from the travel agent:
Name(s) of passenger(s)
Date of departure
Joining point
Name of Travel Agency
Name of caller

In pairs   Task 3

Write down the important details of the holiday for Mr. Wallace, including the cost and when the balance is to be paid, and explain anything else which he is unsure of.

2C   Balance due

When you started at Travel Well Ltd, Mrs. Roper had explained.

'Most tour operators want the balance of the holiday payment no later than 8 weeks before the date of departure. To be on the safe side, we ask for it 9 weeks before, which gives us a week to forward it to the operator. So – 12 weeks before we send the client a postcard to remind them when the final payment date is. If we don't hear from them, then 11 weeks before we send them a letter requesting them to pay the balance. If we still don't receive it, we ring them during the 10th week, asking them if they still want the holiday and emphasizing that the final payment date is only a few days away'.

On the 15th May, Anne, the assistant Manager, comes to you with a client's file and says –

'Give them a ring, would you Susan – and let them know their balance is due'.

You look at the top sheet of the file below and realize that Anne has made an error.

In pairs   Task 1

Simulate telling Anne tactfully, that you think she has made an error.
Information for Anne:
You pride yourself on your efficient and accurate work. When Susan tells you that you have made an error – you do not believe her at first. You are also embarrassed that the error has been pointed out in the shop with other colleagues present.

TRAVEL WELL LTD

Client's name: *Mrs. J. Peters*

Address: *42 Talgarth Close, Barton*

Tour Operator: *Meditours*

Tour No: *9 B 242*

Destination/Resort: *Rigando*

Accomodation: *Hotel Minerva / Single / Twin*

Full (Part Board) Accomodation Only:

No. in party: *3 (1 Adult 2 Children)*

Departure date: *August 7th*

Date of return: *August 21st*

Travel details: *Wingair WG 202 Ex Gatwick 2030*
Return WG 203 1150

Deposit: £ *38*   Received *22nd April*

Balance: £ *342*   due *5th June* Received

Booking taken by *Anne*

On your own   Task 2

Below is the printed postcard you send out after 11 weeks before the departure date. **Write down** what you would put on the card.

TRAVEL WELL LTD
Head Office: 14 Grant Street, Lanchester   525–1321
Barton Branch: 18 High Street, Barton   242–1396
Dear
Yours sincerely,
for Travel Well Ltd

On your own   Task 3

It is now the 24 May and you have heard nothing from Mrs. Peters. **Draft** a letter for Louise to type.

In pairs   Task 4

It is now the 31 May. You **phone** Mrs. Peters.

Information for Mrs. Peters:
You have not received the postcard or letter. You are going away today to visit relatives and you cannot come into the shop until June 7th.

2D A complaint

Mrs. Peters, the client in **2C** did pay for her holiday and has now returned after it. She comes into the shop to make a complaint about it. When you started at Travel Well, the following advice was given about complaints:

1 Be courteous and sympathetic to the client, however aggressive s/he is.
2 Get the client's file.
3 Don't take sides for or against the client or tour operator.
4 Advise the client to write to the tour operator immediately detailing the complaint.
5 Make notes for our reference. Remember to make clear, in your notes, whether the complaint refers to: the Carrier (airline, coach operator etc): the Tour Operator (representative, excursions etc); the Hotel itself; the Resort.
6 If the client is not satisfied, refer him/her to the manager.

In pairs Task 1

Simulate the encounter with Mrs. Peters and **make notes** for your reference.
Information for Mrs. Peters:
You wish to complain about the following:

1 On the outward journey, the flight was delayed for 5 hours.
2 The brochure said the hotel was a mile from the beach. It was more like 3 miles.
3 The beach was polluted.
4 The tour representative never called at your hotel.
5 The food was poor.
6 None of the advertised excursions was available.
7 The paddling pool, mentioned in the brochure, didn't have any water in it.
8 There was no special children's menu as advertised in the brochure.
9 There was poor plumbing in your hotel room: the lavatory kept breaking down; there was no hot water. The walls were paper thin and the smell from the kitchens below was very strong.
10 The hotel staff were rude.

In pairs Task 2

The Managing Director of Travel Well Ltd, Mr. Johnson, likes to be informed immediately about any complaints. **Phone** him with the details of Mrs. Peters' complaint.

Assignments 3

Bendalls Ltd

Bendalls is a department store in the northern city of Manpool. It was established in 1884 and is famous for the quality of its goods and its excellent service. A sales assistant is responsible to the Sales Floor supervisor and through him/her to the Department manager. New sales staff are given a 3-day training programme before going on to the sales floor. They are then attached to an experienced sales assistant for a further two weeks.

3A Starting at Bendalls

You are a new member of staff, Jane Brown. During the initial training programme, great emphasis is put on the importance of approaching customers with a positive attitude.

In groups Task 1

Individuals should **simulate** approaching a customer who is looking at garments on a rail. Bearing in mind Unit 1 Self presentation and non-verbal communication, **discuss** individual approaches.

In pairs Task 2

Overleaf are diagrams of the ground and first floors of Bendalls. Give **precise directions** to customers trying to find the following departments:

a) You are in Menswear. Customer wants Haberdashery.
b) You are in Stationery. Customer wants Menswear.
c) You are in Ladies wear. Customer wants Furniture.
d) You are in Soft furnishings. Customer wants Kitchenware.
e) You are in Books. Customer wants Food.
f) You are in Haberdashery. Customer wants Furniture.
g) You are in Menswear. Customer wants Kitchenware.
h) You are in Food. Customer wants Ladies wear.
i) You are in Furniture. Customer wants Food.
j) You are in Children's clothes. Customer wants Books.

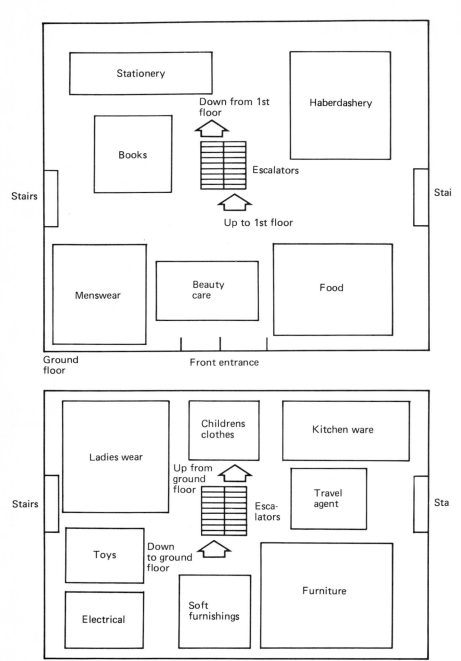

Stationery

Haberdashery

Down from 1st floor

Escalators

Books

Stairs

Stai

Up to 1st floor

Menswear

Beauty care

Food

Ground floor

Front entrance

Ladies wear

Childrens clothes

Kitchen ware

Up from ground floor

Travel agent

Stairs

Esca-lators

Sta

Toys

Down to ground floor

Electrical

Soft furnishings

Furniture

1st floor

You serve your first customer in the Electrical department. You have a Sales Assistant's Guide in which you read the following:

'——Know your product. Consult the Departmental handbook.
——Don't invent information about a product just to complete a sale. If you don't know, ask another assistant or your supervisor'.

The customer is interested in buying a Toolson electric drill. The Departmental Handbook has the following information about this.
'Toolson 143 Electric Drill. Price: £29.40.
Major features:

1 *Speed control*
   Low speed – suitable for: screwdriving, polishing, turning, masonry.
   High speed – suitable for: sawing, sanding, hedge-trimming, grinding.
2 *Double insulation*
   All the external metal parts are insulated from the mains electricity supply.
3 *Hammer action*
   For drilling hard masonry. Special drill bits are needed for this.
4 *Attachments* (extra)
   a) Finishing sander   £6.30
   b) Circular saw   £7.90

Information for the customer:
You particularly want to know the following about the Toolson Electric Drill.

a)   Does it have more than one speed?
b)   Are the metal parts insulated?
c)   What do you use to drill through plaster? How do you drill glass and metal?

(*) Tasks 3–5 will require 3 group members, only two of whom are involved in a simulation at any one time.

In pairs   Task 3

Simulate the sale.

Task 4

You don't have some of the information the customer requires. You go over to your supervisor. **Simulate** the conversation.
Information for supervisor:

a)   *Drilling plaster*. A masonry drill bit is necessary. The hammer action should not be used.
b)   *Drilling glass*. You should use a spear point drill bit. The glass should have a firm, flat backing. A small ring of putty or plasticine should be put round the point to be drilled and filled with paraffin to cool the

drill bit. (Use water when drilling a mirror). Only start the drill after applying it to the work.

c) *Drilling metal.* You should use a twist drill made of high speed steel. Use oil as a cutting lubricant on all metal except cast iron and brass. When drilling aluminium, use paraffin. Drill a pilot hole before a longer hole. Use the High Speed with small drill bits; the Slow Speed with large drill bits.

In pairs   Task 5

You return to the customer, convey the information to him/her and complete the sale.

3B   Stationery

You are now at the end of your two week training period and are transferred to the Stationery department. When you are low on stock, you complete a Stock Order Form like the one below. You take this to the Stationery Stock Room and leave it with the stock room assistant who then brings the stock to the department. Mr. Reeves, your supervisor, asks you to fill in a stock sheet:—

'Jane – we're running a bit low on some things. We need 2 more boxes of HB pencils and those felt tip pens are moving fast – let's have a dozen of each of the black medium tip, black fine tip and red medium. Oh – and don't forget a box of H pencils. And – envelopes – yes – one box of the Manilla A4 – that's the extra strong variety, one box of the small white and then paper: 10 pads lined A4; 20 of the foolscap lined and 5 unlined A4 pads. That'll do.'

On your own   Task 1

Write down the information you would use to complete the Stock Order Form.

BENDALLS LTD
STOCK ORDER FORM
Department:

Product	Variety/type/description	Quantity

You take the form to the stationery stock room and give it to Peter, the stockroom assistant. After 10 minutes, Peter hasn't brought the stock you requested. During staff training, the importance of good relations between sales staff and stockroom staff was stressed.

Your supervisor says –

'Jane – where's that stock? We're getting very low. Nip along and see what Peter's up to – will you?'

In pairs   Task 2

Simulate the conversation between Peter and yourself when you return to the stock room.

Information for Peter:

Your stock room supervisor asked you to do some important stocktaking. He will be returning soon to see that it has been done. You are not terribly happy doing your job. You would prefer to be a sales assistant. You don't take kindly to sales staff of the same seniority as yourself, particularly new staff, commenting on how you do your job.

In pairs   Task 3

Peter does deliver the stock to your department. You check it and find he has delivered the following –

HB pencils	1 box
H pencils	2 boxes
Black pens – fine tip	12
Black pens – medium tip	12
Small white envelopes	3 boxes
A4 lined pads	20
Foolscap lined pads	10
A4 unlined pads	10

You go back to the stockroom and inform Peter of his error. **Simulate** the situation.

3C   A complaint

You have now been working for Bendalls for 6 months and are working in Ladies wear. The Sales Assistant's Guide says the following about complaints.

' – Try to deal with a complaint yourself. But if a customer is not satisfied, call your supervisor.

– Remember – customers making complaints are sometimes aggressive and upset. Be courteous at all times.

– If the item is damaged, try to discover whether it was damaged when it was bought or afterwards, without giving the customer the impression that you are accusing them of something.'

Your supervisor, Mrs. Leslie, tells you –

'If the garment is damaged, ask the customer what happened: have they worn it? Have they washed it? If so – how?

An angry customer comes in to complain about a cardigan she bought the previous Saturday, which has stretched. You look at the receipt and discover it was sold by a Saturday–only assistant. The label on the cardigan is the one below.

(*) Tasks 1 and 2 will require 3 group members, only two of whom are involved in a simulation at any one time.

TO FIT 36"
BUST

60%   Lambswool
20%   Angora
20%   Nylon

Warm Hand Wash
Do **NOT** rub or wring
DRY FLAT away from direct
heat and sunlight

RESHAPE while damp

In pairs   Task 1

Simulate the complaint.
Information for the customer:
You bought the cardigan the previous Saturday. The assistant who served you did not warn you it might stretch. You gave it a warm wash in your washing machine and then hung it on a coat hanger to dry.
You are very angry because you considered the cardigan to be expensive.

In pairs   Task 2

Explain the situation to her in front of the customer.
(The customer is not satisfied. You call Mrs. Leslie over.)

Mrs. Leslie thinks Bendalls are not responsible and the customer's complaint not justified. But the customer leaves, intending to complain to the General manager and particularly about how Mrs. Leslie and yourself have treated her. In such situations, it is usual to write a report describing the complaint and what happened during the encounter with the customer.

On your own   Task 3

Mrs. Leslie asks you to **draft** the report.